TEACI
JAI

PREM MOTWANI
&
NORIKO NASUKAWA

A Sterling Paperback

STERLING PAPERBACKS
An imprint of
Sterling Publishers (P) Ltd.
A-59, Okhla Industrial Area, Phase-II, New Delhi-110020
Ph. : 26387070, 26386209, Fax : 91-11- 26383788
E-mail : ghai@nde.vsnl.net.in
Website: www.sterlingpublishers.com

Teach Yourself Japanese
©1998, Prem Motwani & Noriko Nasukawa
ISBN 81 207 2081 4
Reprint 1999, 2001, 2003, 2005, 2006

Published by Sterling Publishers Pvt. Ltd., New Delhi-110020.
Lasertypeset by Vikas Compographics, New Delhi-110020.
Printed at Sterling Publishers Pvt. Ltd., New Delhi-110020.

PREFACE

It is a popular myth that Japanese Language is difficult for foreigners to learn. It is essentially because Japanese orthography is a unique mixture of three scripts, Hiragana, Katakana and Kanji, making it a herculian task to master even for the Japanese themselves. However, Japanese grammar and pronunciation are not necessarily very difficult.

In recent years there has been widespread demand for learning only the spoken language, minus the script. Hence there have been a large number of books that provide instant communication through situational conversation. This all-romanized book, however, follows an all grammar approach aiming at providing the reader a sound grounding in basic grammar in a short span of time (approximately 100 to 125 hours), while still laying maximum emphasis on conversational skills. Further, in order to facilitate self-study, lots of annotations, drills, with a key to solutions, new vocabulary in each chapter and a complete audio-tape have been provided. A complete index has also been provided for easy reference both from English as well as Japanese. Moreover, an appendix containing classified vocabulary on a wide variety of subjects has been provided to enable further in-depth study. Sentences and phrases that are most commonly used by the Japanese in daily life have been selected, based on the long experience of the authors of teaching Japanese to foreigners. In sum, elementary and intermediate Japanese have been condensed into one and hence the scope of this book is not limited to the casual learner or traveller to Japan, but it should prove to be a good stepping stone for those who wish to build a sound base for handling the language in both written and spoken situations without any outside guidance.

PRONUNCIATION

- See the syllabary chart.
- Japanese has no stress accent like in English. Each syllable is given equal stress but it has a high-low pitch system.
- There are 5 syllables in Japanese and a is pronounced as *ah*, i as *ee*, u as *oo*, e as eh and o as *oh*.
- The consonants are *k, s, sh, t, ch, ts, h, f, m, r, g, j, z, d, b* and *p*. Except n, there is no single consonant in Japanese. All consonants are either a combination of one consonant and one short vowel or double consonant and a short vowel.
- The *u* is frequently silent at the end of a word as in *desu* and *masu*.
- Macron mark (-) on *o* and *u* implies the elongation or the prolonged sound.

  Compare Kyo and Kyō, Shu and Shū.

HOW TO USE THIS BOOK

1. Read each chapter carefully taking note of finer grammatical details given in each lesson.
2. Attempt 'Try these' before proceeding on to the next part or chapter. Use 'Key to solutions' only as the last resort.
3. Vocabulary used in each chapter has been given at the end of the same. Memorizing the vocabulary is the most important aspect of language learning.
4. Preferably revise the previous few chapters before attempting a new one.
5. Counting, classifiers, adjectives, conjugation of verbs, transitive and intransitive verbs have been included in the Appendices (Part I), but study them carefully when you encounter them for the first time.

ABOUT THE AUDIO TAPES

1. Audio tapes contain only the basic lessons from Chapter 1 to 54 and greetings in Japanese.
2. Always listen to the audio tape first when attempting a new chapter.
3. Serial number of sentences in each lesson has been said in Japanese i.e., ichi (for 1), ni (for 2), san (for 3) and so on. For counting, see Appendices Part I.
4. In case there are 2 options in a sentence such as affirmative and negative forms (latter in brackets), only the first option has been included in the audio-tape.

SYLLABRY CHART

LIST OF HIRAGANA

あ	a	い	i	う	u	え	e	お	o
か	k a	き	k i	く	k u	け	k e	こ	k o
さ	s a	し	s h i	す	s u	せ	s e	そ	s o
た	t a	ち	c h i	つ	t s u	て	t e	と	t o
な	n a	に	n i	ぬ	n u	ね	n e	の	n o
は	h a	ひ	h i	ふ	f u	へ	h e	ほ	h o
ま	m a	み	m i	む	m u	め	m e	も	m o
や	y a	(い)	(i)	ゆ	y u	(え)	(e)	よ	y o
ら	r a	り	r i	る	r u	れ	r e	ろ	r o
わ	w a	(い)	(i)	(う)	(u)	(え)	(e)	を	o
ん	n								

ga	が	gi	ぎ	gu	ぐ	ge	げ	go	ご
za	ざ	ji	じ	zu	ず	ze	ぜ	zo	ぞ
da	だ	ji	ぢ	zu	づ	de	で	do	ど
ba	ば	bi	び	bu	ぶ	be	べ	bo	ぼ
pa	ぱ	pi	ぴ	pu	ぷ	pe	ぺ	po	ぽ

kya	きゃ	kyu	きゅ	kyo	きょ
sha	しゃ	shu	しゅ	sho	しょ
cha	ちゃ	chu	ちゅ	cho	ちょ
nya	にゃ	nyu	にゅ	nyo	にょ
hya	ひゃ	hyu	ひゅ	hyo	ひょ
mya	みゃ	myu	みゅ	myo	みょ
rya	りゃ	ryu	りゅ	ryo	りょ

gya	ぎゃ	gyu	ぎゅ	gyo	ぎょ
ja	じゃ	ju	じゅ	jo	じょ

bya	びゃ	byu	びゅ	byo	びょ
pya	ぴゃ	pyu	ぴゅ	pyo	ぴょ

LIST OF KATAKANA

	a	ア	i	イ	u	ウ	e	エ	o	オ
k	ka	カ	ki	キ	ku	ク	ke	ケ	ko	コ
s	sa	サ	shi	シ	su	ス	se	セ	so	ソ
t	ta	タ	chi	チ	tsu	ツ	te	テ	to	ト
n	na	ナ	ni	ニ	nu	ヌ	ne	ネ	no	ノ
h	ha	ハ	hi	ヒ	fu	フ	he	ヘ	ho	ホ
m	ma	マ	mi	ミ	mu	ム	me	メ	mo	モ
y	ya	ヤ	(i)	(イ)	yu	ユ	(e)	(エ)	yo	ヨ
r	ra	ラ	ri	リ	ru	ル	re	レ	ro	ロ
w	wa	ワ	(i)	(イ)	(u)	ウ	(e)	(エ)	o	ヲ
	n	ン								

ga	ガ	gi	ギ	gu	グ	ge	ゲ	go	ゴ
za	ザ	ji	ジ	zu	ズ	ze	ゼ	zo	ソ
da	ダ	ji	ヂ	zu	ヅ	de	デ	do	ド
ba	バ	bi	ビ	bu	ブ	be	ベ	bo	ボ
pa	パ	pi	ピ	pu	プ	pe	ペ	po	ポ

kya	キャ	kyu	キュ	kyo	キョ
sha	シャ	shu	シュ	sho	ショ
cha	チャ	chu	チュ	cho	チョ
nya	ニャ	nyu	ニュ	nyo	ニョ
hya	ヒャ	hyu	ヒュ	hyo	ヒョ
mya	ミャ	myu	ミュ	myo	ミョ
rya	リャ	ryu	リュ	ryo	リョ

gya	ギャ	gyu	ギュ	gyo	ギョ
ja	ジャ	ju	ジュ	jo	ジョ

bya	ビャ	byu	ビュ	byo	ビョ
pya	ピャ	pyu	ピュ	pyo	ピョ

CONTENTS

1
DESU

Lesson

1.	*Kore wa hon desu.*	-This is a book.
2.	*Sore wa hon desu ka.*	-Is that a book?
	Hai, sō desu.	-Yes, it is.
	Iie, sō dewa arimasen.	-No, it isn't.
3.	*Kore wa hon dewa arimasen.*	-This isn't a book.
4.	*Kore wa hon dewa arimasen ka.*	-Isn't this a book?
5.	*Are mo hon desu ka.*	-Is that also a book?
6.	*Kore wa nan desu ka.*	-What is this?
	(Sore wa) Nōto desu.	-(That is) a notebook.
7.	*Kore wa hon desu ka, nōto desu ka.*	

-Is this a book or a notebook?

(Sore wa) hon desu.   -(That is) a book.

8.	*Kore wa watashi no hon desu.*	-This is my book.
9.	*Sore wa anata no nōto desu ka.*	-It that your notebook?
10.	*Kore wa dare no nōto desu ka?*	-Whose notebook is this?

(Sore wa) Tanaka san no (nōto) desu.

-(That is) Mr. Tanaka's (note book).

11. *Dore ga watashi no (nōto) desu ka.*

- Which is mine? (my notebook)

12. *Kore wa hon de sore wa jisho desu.*

-This is a book, and that is a dictionary.

13. *Kyō wa getsuyōbi de ashita wa kayōbi desu.*
     -Today is Monday, and tomorrow is Tuesday.

14. *Kyō wa shigoto de ashita wa yasumi desu.*
     -Today is working day, and tomorrow is holiday.

Grammar

Kore .... This	
Sore .... That	
Are .... That one over there	
Dore .... Which	

These are demonstratives in Japanese and are always followed by subject particle 'wa' (in case of interrogative demonstrative, always 'ga'). Their use depends on the distance of the object from the speaker.

desu .... is, are

It is the copula and always used at the end of a sentence after a noun or adjective (see Chapter 2). Negative form of 'desu' is 'dewa arimasen'.

Two sentences ending with noun+'desu' are joined by converting 'desu' into 'de'.

Particles (all particles in Japanese are post positional) wa / ga

These are subject particles and each subject in a sentence must be followed by 'wa'('ga' is used for more emphasis as in case of interrogative words as subject).

mo .... also

It replaces subject particle 'wa' or 'ga'.

no ....'s (possesive)

It is always used between 2 nouns where the former modifies the latter e.g. watashi no (mine), dare no (whose)

Noun following 'no' may be dropped if the object in question is in front of the speaker and listener or known by both.

ka	-	interrogative particle

An interrogative sentence must end in 'ka'.

Try these I :
1. Kore wa _____ *Kamera* _____ desu ka.
   kamera/ terebi/ isu
   - Hai sō desu.
   - Iie sō dewa arimasen.

2. Sore wa _____ *watashi* _____ no kaban desu ka.
   anata/ watashi/ Suzuki san/ dare

3. Are wa nan desu ka.
   _____ *jisho* _____ desu.
   tokei/ kaban/ jisho/ shinbun

4. Kore wa _____ *hon* _____ desu ka, _____ *jisho* _____ desu ka.
   hon   / jisho
   enpitsu / pen
   shinbun / zasshi

Other demonstratives:

1. Koko (wa)   this place
   Soko (wa)   that place
   Asoko (wa)   that place (over there)
   Doko (ga)   where (which place)

Note :
This set of demonstratives is exclusively used for place and their application is same as 'kore' 'sore' 'are' 'dore', except that the noun used is also invariably related to a place.

- Koko wa jimusho desu.   - This is an (the) office.
- Soko wa toire desu.   - That is the toilet.
- Asoko wa nan desu ka.   - What is that place?
- Doko ga SONY no mise desu ka. - Where is SONY's shop?

2.
Kochira	-	this way, this side
Sochira	-	that way, that side
Achira	-	there, overthere
Dochira	-	where, which side

Note:

This set of demonstratives is primarily used for direction and their application is same as above mentioned two sets of demonstratives.

This set has wider application such as it can be used in place of 'koko', 'soko', 'asoko', 'doko', but in such a case this set is more polite, and it can be used for introducing a person pointing towards the direction he/she is sitting or standing or when asking or showing the direction to a senior person.

- Toire wa dochira desu ka. - Where is the toilet? (which side)
  - Achira desu.   - Overthere.
  (kochira/sochira)   (this side/that side)
- Kochira wa Yamada san desu. - This side is Mr. Yamada.
  (sochira/achira)   (that side/overthere)

-
Kono	-	this
Sono	-	that
Ano	-	that one overthere
Dono	-	which one

Note :

This set of demonstratives has exactly same meaning as 'kore', 'sore', 'are', 'dore' except that this set must be followed by a noun and then particle 'wa' or 'ga' as the case may be.

- Kono hon wa watashi no (hon) desu.

  - This book is mine.
  (my book)

- Sono kaban wa dare no (kaban) desu ka.

  - Whose bag is that?

4

- Ano uchi wa Yamada san no (uchi) desu ka.
  - Is that house overthere Mr. Yamada's (house)?

- Dono kasa ga anata no (kasa) desu ka.
  - Which one is your umbrella?

Try these II :
1. Koko wa _Tanaka san no uchi_ desu ka.
   Tanaka san no uchi/uketsuke/kyōshitsu.
   - Hai, sō desu.
   - Iie, (koko wa) _Tanaka san no uchi_ dewa arimasen.
   (koko wa) _Suzuki san no uchi_ desu.
   Suzuki san no uchi/ uriba/ jimusho

2. Soko wa _resutoran_ desu.
   māketto/ resutoran/ tokeiya

3. Asoko wa nan desu ka.
   - (Asoko wa) _watashi no kaisha_ desu.
   kūkō/ eki/ watashi no kaisha

4. Doko ga _yaoya_ desu ka.
   uketsuke/ yaoya/ basutei

Vocabulary

(Tanaka san no)uchi	Mr.Tanaka's house
anata	you
bōrupen	ball point pen
basutei	bus stop
dare	who
denwa	telephone
depāto	department store
eki	station
enpitsu	pencil
hai	yes
hon	book
iie	no
isu	chair
jisho	dictionary
kūkō	airport
kaban	bag
kaisha	company
kamera	camera
kuruma	car

kyōshitsu .... class room
māketto .... market
nōto .... notebook
nan .... what
pen .... pen
resutoran .... restaurant
sō .... so
sūpā .... super market
san .... Mr, Ms.
senpūki .... fan
shinbun .... newspaper
tabako .... cigarette
terebi .... T.V.
tokei .... watch, clock
tokeiya .... watchmaker
tokoya .... barber
tsukue .... table, desk
uketsuke .... reception
uriba .... counter
watashi I
yaoya .... vegetable store
zasshi .... magazine

2
ADJECTIVES

(1) I-adjectives

Lesson

1. *Kore wa yasui desu.*   -This is cheap.
2. *Sore wa ii desu.*   -That is good.
3. *Are wa (chotto) furui desu.*   -That is (little) old.
4. *Dore ga yasui desu ka.*   -Which one is cheap?
5. *Koko wa (taihen) samui desu.*   -This place is (very) cold.
6. *Soko wa hiroi desu.*   -That place is spacious.
7. *Asoko wa (ichiban) takai desu.*
      -That place is (most) expensive.
8. *Doko ga omoshiroi desu ka.*
      -Which place is interesting?
9. *Kono hon wa (sukoshi) muzukashii desu.*
      -This book is slightly difficult.
10. *Sono heya wa semai desu.*   -That room is small.
11. *Ano kuruma wa hayai desu.*   -That car is fast.
12. *Dono kaban ga karui desu ka.*   -Which bag is light?

Negative form: Last 'i' turns into 'kunai'.

1. *Kore wa (amari) yasuku nai desu.*
      -This is not (so) cheap.
2. *Kono hon wa (zenzen) muzukashiku nai desu.*
      -This book is not (at all) difficult.

Past tense: Last 'i' turns into 'katta'.
1. *Asoko wa takakatta desu.*   -That place was expensive.

2. *Ano kuruma wa hayakatta desu.*   -That car was fast.

Past Negative form: Last 'i' turns into 'ku nakatta'.
1. *Kono hon wa muzukashiku nakatta desu.*
                             -This book wasn't difficult.

2. *Asoko wa takaku nakatta desu.*
                             -That place wasn't expensive.

Conjunctive form: (joining two i-adjectives that complement each other) 'i' of the preceding adjective turns into 'kute'.

1. *Koko (kono heya) wa hirokute akarui desu.*
         -This place (this room) is spacious and bright.

2. *Asoko (ano resutoran) wa takakute mazui desu.*
                    -That place (that restaurant) is expensive and unpalatable.

Probability form: 'Desu' turns to deshō.
1. *Indo wa atsui deshō.*   -India must be hot.

2. *Nihon wa takakatta deshō.*
                    -Japan must have been expensive.

Grammar:

There are two types of adjectives in Japanese. I-adjectives are so called as they invariably end in vowel + 'i' (yasui, hayai, furui, etc.)

The other type does not have a fixed ending, and are called Na-adjectives. To be more precise, adjectives that do not end in vowel + 'i' (exceptions: kirei, kirai, yūmei, yukai, fuyukai, tokui) are Na-adjectives. They are so called as particle 'na' must be added between adjective and the noun.

Additional exceptions:
1. ōkii (big)   chiisai (small)
These are so called i-adjectives but colloquially, can also take 'na' when followed by a noun.
e.g.) ōkii kuni or ōkina kuni (big country)

2. 'ii' (good) is always 'yoi' when conjugated
    e.g.)   yokunai   (negative)
             yokatta   (past)
             yokunakatta   (past negative)
             yokute   (conjunctive)

Adverbs:
'Chotto,' 'taihen,' 'sukoshi' are some of the adverbs used in affirmative sentences while 'amari' and 'zenzen' are mostly used in negative sentences. 'ichiban' is used for the superlative degree.

Try these:

1. Kore wa taihen _____ desu.
        amai / oishii / nagai

2. Are wa chotto _____ desu.
            nigai / tsumetai / hosoi (make past tense)

3. Soko wa amari _____ desu.
        atarashii / chikai / atsui

4. Sono ryōri wa zenzen _____ desu.
            karai / oishii / takai (make past negative)

5. Ano resutoran wa _____, _____ desu.
            yasui   oishii

6. Kono heya wa _____, _____ desu.
            semai   kurai

1. Comparison of two things: (dochira ga ii desu ka)

1. Kōhī to kōcha to dochira ga ii desu ka.
                        -Which do you prefer, coffee or tea?
    - Kōhī no hō ga ii desu.   -I prefer coffee.

2. Tokyo to Nyūyōku to dochira ga ōkii desu ka.
                        -Which one is bigger, Tokyo or New York?

    - (Nyūyōku yori) Tokyo no hō ga okii desu.
                        -Tokyo is bigger (than New York).

9

3. Hikōki to shinkansen to dochira ga hayai desu ka.

> -Which is faster, airplane or Shinkansen? (bullet train)

- Mochiron hikōki no hō ga hayai desu.

> Of course, airplane is faster.

2. Comparison of more than two things : (dore ga ii desu ka)

1. Kōhī to kōcha to jūsu no naka de dore ga ii desu ka.

> -Which do you prefer, coffee, tea or juice?

- Jūsu ga ii desu   -I prefer juice.

2. Nihongo to eigo to furansugo no naka de dore ga (ichiban) muzukashii desu ka.

> -Which is (most) difficult, Japanese, English or French?

- Nihongo ga (ichiban) muzukashii desu.

> - Japanese is (most) difficult.

Vocabulary

akarui	bright
amai	sweet
amari(nai)	not so
atarashii	new
atsui	hot
chikai	near
chotto	little
eigo	English
furansugo	French
furui	old
go (suffix)	language
hayai	fast
heya	room
hikōki	airplane
hiroi	spacious
hosoi	thin
ichiban	most
ii (yoi)	good
jūsu	juice
kōcha	tea
kōhī	coffee
karai	spicy
karui	light
kurai	dark

```
mazui ............................................. unpalatable
mochiron ....................................... of course
muzukashii .................................... difficult
nagai ............................................. long
nigai ............................................. bitter
Nihon ............................................ Japan
nihongo ......................................... Japanese (language)
Nyūyōku ........................................ New York
oishii ............................................ delicious
omoshiroi ...................................... interesting
ryōri ............................................. dish
samui ............................................ cold weather
semai ............................................ small, cramped
sukoshi ......................................... slightly
taihen ........................................... very
takai ............................................ expensive/high
tsumetai ....................................... chilly, cold (object)
yasui ............................................ cheap
zenzen nai ..................................... not at all
```

3
(2) NA-ADJECTIVES

Lesson
1. *Kanojo wa kirei desu.*   -She is beautiful.
2. *Kare wa eigo ga jōzu desu.*   -He is good at English.
3. *Kare wa hade na hito desu.*
                              -He is a flamboyant person.
4. *Koko wa benri na tokoro desu.*
                              -This is a convenient place.

Negative form: Na-adjectives have same conjugation as noun + desu as in Lesson 1, i.e., desu is always conjugated.
1. *Kanojo wa amari kirei dewa arimasen.*
                              -She is not so beautiful.
2. *Kare wa eigo ga jōzu dewa arimasen.*
                              -He is not good at English.

Past tense: 'desu' turns to 'deshita'
1. *Kare wa taihen shinsetsu deshita.*
                              -He was very kind.
2. *Kanojo wa nihongo ga heta deshita*
                    -She was not good at Japanese.

Past negative form: 'Desu' turns to 'dewa arimasen deshita'.
1. *Ano hito wa (zenzen) yūmei dewa arimasen deshita.*
                    -That person was not famous (at all).
2. *Asoko wa (amari) shizuka dewa arimasen deshita.*
                    -That place was not (so) quiet.

Probability form: 'Desu' turns to 'deshō'.
1. *Asoko wa fuben deshō.*
   -That place must be inconvenient.
2. *Nihonjin wa shinsetsu deshō.*
   -You must have found Japanese to be polite.

Conjunctive form: 'Desu' turns to 'de'.
   i.e. 'de' is used between two adjectives.

Notes: If i-adjective and na-adjective are to be joined, they are joined with 'kute' if the first adjective is i-adjective and with 'de' if it is na-adjective.
Same rule is applicable if there are more than two adjectives. Note the applications given below.

1. Kanojo wa kirei de sumāto desu.
   -She is beautiful and slim.
2. Kono tsukue wa ōkikute jōbu desu.
   -This table is big and sturdy.
3. Sono pen wa karukute benri de ii desu.
   -That pen is light, handy and good.

Grammar: As stated earlier na-adjectives do not have a fixed ending and hence adjectives from foreign languages specially English all fall under this category. For example,
popyurā (popular), shinpuru (simple)
unīku (unique), karafuru (colorful)
modan (modern), etc..

Many na-adjectives take particle 'ga' before them, such as 'suki' 'kirai' 'heta' 'hoshii'(i-adj.).

Try these:
1. Watashi wa nihon ryōri ga _____ desu.
                              suki / kirai

2. Kare wa _____ na hito desu.
   ,   iya / shinsetsu / genki

13

3. Kore wa _____ dewa arimasen.
   hitsuyō / taisetsu / fukuzatsu

4. Are wa _____ deshita.
   zannen / fushigi / kiken

5. Tokyo wa amari _____ dewa arimasen deshita.
   shizuka / fuben

6. Kono hito wa _____ de _____ desu.
   shinsetsu / yukai,
   yasashii / omoshiroi

Vocabulary

benri	convenient
fuben	inconvenient
fukuzatsu	complicated
fushigi	strange
genki	cheerful
hade	flamboyant
hito	person
hitsuyō	necessary
iya	unpleasant
jōbu	sturdy
kanojo	she
kare	he
kiken	dangerous
kirai	dislike
kirei	beautiful
nihonjin	Japanese (people)
omoshiroi	interesting
shinsetsu	kind
shizuka	quiet
suki	like
sumāto	smart
taisetsu	important
yūmei	famous
yasashii	gentle
yukai	jolly
zannen	unfortunate

4
VERBS (1)

Lesson
Verbs of existance (arimasu, imasu) ('masu' pronounced as 'mas')

1) Arimasu
Existance of inanimate (non-living things)

1. *Kyō no shinbun ga arimasu ka.*
   -Do you have today's newspaper?
   - *Hai, arimasu.*   -Yes, I have.
   - *Iie, arimasen.*   -No, I don't have.

2. *Kaigi wa itsu arimasu ka.*
   -When is the meeting?
   - *Ashita arimasu.* (colloquially *desu.*)
   -Tomorrow.

3. *Kono heya ni nani ga arimasu ka.*
   -What is there in this room?
   - *Iroiro na mono ga arimasu.*
   -There are various things.

4. *Fairu wa tsukue no ue ni arimasu.*
   -File is on the table.

5. *Tāji Mahāru wa doko ni arimasu ka.*
   -Where is Taj Mahal?
   - *Indo ni arimasu.*   -It is in India.

Negative form: 'masu' turns to 'masen'
   Ima jikan ga arimasen.   -I don't have time now.

Past tense: 'masu' turns to 'mashita'
   Kesa jishin ga arimashita.
   -There was an earthquake this morning.

15

Past negative form: 'masu' turns to 'masen deshita'

Tsukue no shita ni kaban ga arimasen deshita.

-Bag wasn't there under the table.

2) Imasu

Existance of animate (living things)

1. *Ima watashi wa kaisha ni imasu.*

   -I am now in my office.

2. *Anata no uchi ni petto ga imasu ka.*

   -Do you have a pet in your house?

3. *Ano heya ni dare ga imasu ka.*

   -Who is there in that room?

   -Tanaka san to Yamada San ga imasu.

   -Mr. Tanaka and Mr. Yamada are there.

4. *Hayashi san wa soto ni imasu.*

   -Mr. Hayashi is outside.

Negative form: 'masu' turns to 'masen'

Tanaka san wa ima koko ni imasen.

- Mr. Tanaka is not here at the moment.

Past tense: 'masu' turns to 'mashita'.

Yamada san wa sakki made koko ni imashita.

- Mr. Yamada was here a little while ago.

Past negative form: 'masu' turns to 'masendeshita'.

Tanaka san wa soto ni imasen deshita.

- Mr. Tanaka was not to be found outside.

Grammar:

1. 'Arimasu' (dictionary form 'aru') as stated earlier is used for inanimate things, not only physical, but also abstract. For example, 'jikan ga arimasu '(have time), 'kankei ga arimasen '(have no relation), 'genki ga arimasen deshita' (was not in high spirits) etc.

   If the subject comes at the beginning of a sentence followed by, say, place of existence and 'arimasu' at the end, particle 'wa' is used and if place of existence comes at the beginning with subject followed by 'arimasu', mostly 'ga' is used.

   e.g.) Hon *wa* tsukue no ue ni arimasu.

   Tsukue no ue ni hon *ga* arimasu.

16

2. Existance Particle 'ni'

Particle 'ni' is used after the place of existance.

e.g., kono heya ni (in this room)
- no ue ni (on top of)
- no shita ni (beneath)
- no naka ni (inside)
- no migi ni (to the right of)
- no hidari ni (to the left of)
- no mae ni (in front of)
- no ushiro ni (behind)
- no soba ni (nearby, next to) etc.

Particles 'kara' (from), 'made' (upto, till)

1. Kare wa kinō *kara* genki ga arimasen
   -He is not in high spirits since yesterday.

2. Sakki *made* - till a little while ago

Particle 'to' (and) is used for joining two nouns only.
Note: It is never used to join two sentences.

Try these:

1. Denwa wa uketsuke _____ arimasu.
   no mae ni / no soba ni

2. Kinō _____ ga arimasen deshita.
   (denwa / kaigi / jikan)

   (select the appropriate word and form)

3. Kinō no pāti wa hito ga amari _____.
   (imasendeshita,
   arimasendeshita)

4. Kyō wa okane ga zenzen _____.
   (imasen, arimasen)

Vocabulary

ashita	....	tomorrow
fairu	....	file
ima	....	now
Indo	....	India
iroiro	....	various
jikan	....	time
jishin	....	earthquake

kaigi	meeting
kesa	this morning
kyō	today
mono	thing
petto	pet
sakki	a little while ago
shita	under
soto	outside
uchi	house
ue	on

5
VERBS (2)

Lesson
Type 1
1. *Watashi wa ashita Tokyo e ikimasu.*
   -I will go to Tokyo tomorrow.
2. *Watashi wa ku-ji kara go-ji made hatarakimasu.*
   -I work from 9 a.m. to 5 p.m.
3. *(Watashi wa) ichi-ji kara ichi-ji han made yasumimasu.*
   -I have a break from1 p.m. to 1: 30 p.m.
4. *Watashi wa mainichi oyogimasu.*
   -I swim everyday.
5. *(Anata wa) maiban nan-ji ni uchi e kaerimasu ka.*
   -What time do you return home every evening?
6. *(Anata wa) itsu kono hon o kaeshimasu ka.*
   -When will you return this book?

Negative form: 'masu' turns to 'masen'
1. *Watashi wa mada kaerimasen.*
   -I will not go back for some more time.
2. *Watashi wa ongaku o zenzen kikimasen*
   -I don't listen to music at all.

Past tense: 'masu' turns to 'mashita'
1. *(Anata wa) mō te o araimashita ka.*
   -Have you already washed your hands?
2. *Watashi wa sake o hotondo nomimasen.*
   -I hardly ever drink (alcohol).

Past negative: 'masu' turns to 'masendeshita'
1. *Watashi wa kinō pāti ni ikimasen deshita.*
   -I didn't go to the party yesterday.
2. *Watashi wa tegami o kakimasen deshita.*
   - I didn't write the letter.

Type 2
1. *Watashi wa maiasa roku-ji ni okimasu.*
   -I get up at six o'clock every morning.
2. *(Watashi wa) sanjuppun gurai terebi o mimasu.*
   -I watch television for about 30 minutes.
3. *Watashi wa kyō zutto uchi ni imasu.*
   -I'm at home throughout the day.

Negative form: 'masu' turns to 'masen'
Watashi wa sono Kaisha o yamemasen.
   -I'll not leave that company.

Past tense: 'masu' turns to 'mashita'
(Watashi wa) sono eiga o mō mimashita
   -I've already seen that movie.

Past negative: 'masu' turns to 'masen deshita'
Kare wa heya ni imasen deshita.
   -He was not in the room.

Type 3
1. *Anata wa kono ato nani o shimasu ka.*
   -What will you do after this?
2. *Watashi wa korekara nihongo o benkyō shimasu.*
   -I will study Japanese from now on.
3. *Ashita nanji ni kimasu ka.*
   -What time will you come tomorrow?

Negative Form: 'masu' turns to 'masen'
1. *Watashi wa ano mise de kaimono o shimasen.*
   -I do not do shopping at that shop.
2. *Kare wa pāti ni kimasen.* -He will not come to the party.

Past Tense: 'masu' turns to 'mashita'.
1. *Anata wa itsu kekkon shimashita ka.*
-When did you get married?
2. *Kanojo wa koko ni kimashita ka.* -Did she come here?

Past negative: 'masu' turns to 'masen deshita'.
1. *Kare wa shukudai o shimasen deshita.*
-He did not do his homework.
2. *Kanojo wa koko ni kimasen deshita.*
-She did not come here.

Grammar: Types of verbs in Japanese

Type 1:   Always end in 'u' sound in dictionary form but never in 'eru' or 'iru',
e.g.) 'au' (to meet), 'noru' (to board), 'okosu' (to wake someone up), sumu (to live) etc. (exceptions 'hairu (to enter), 'kaeru' (to return), 'hashiru (to run), 'shiru' (to know), 'iru' (to need), 'kiru' (to cut) etc.

Type 2:   Always end in 'eru' 'iru' sound.
e.g.) 'taberu' (to eat), 'miru' (to see), 'oriru' (to alight), 'kariru' (to borrow), 'yameru' (to give up), 'iru' (to be) etc.

Type 3:   There are only two verbs in this category, namely 'suru' (to do) and 'kuru' (to come). They are placed in a separate category as they follow different conjugation than type 1 verbs.

'Masu' form All verbs must be put in 'masu' form, specially in the spoken language as it is the polite form.

Type 1:   Convert last 'u' into 'i' and add 'masu'.
(exceptions: tatsu (to stand) → tachimasu
hanasu (to speak) → hanashimasu

Type 2:   Drop final 'ru' and add 'masu'
e.g.) 'taberu' → 'tabemasu'
'miru' → 'mimasu'
'okiru' (to get up) → 'okimasu'

Type 3:   Since it has special form, it must be remembered
           by heart.
           e.g) 'suru' → 'shimasu'
                'kuru' → 'kimasu'

Once 'masu' form is obtained negative, past and past
negative can be easily obtained as described in the lesson

Particles:
e: directional particle (implies the direction)
    e.g.) Tokyo   e   ikimasu.
           Uchi   e   kaerimasu.
           Koko   e   kimasu

ni: time particle (when specifying time)
    e.g.) 2 ji ni (at 2 o'clock)
           nan ji ni (at what time)

o: direct object particle (used after the noun which is the direct
    object of a verb)
    e.g.) Hon o kaeshimasu.
           Tegami o kakimasu.

Adverbs:
mada: (not yet)
           The verb following it must always be put in the
           negative form as it implies that an action has not
           yet taken place. However it is also used in
           affirmative sentences.
           e.g. '~wa mada desu' (~is yet to be done)

hotondo:1) (hardly, almost never)
           It is mostly used in negative sentences.
           Hotondo tabemasen deshita.
                                   -I hardly ate anything.

        2) (almost all)
           It can also be used in affirmative sentences.
           Hotondo tabemashita.
                                   -I have almost eaten (finished) all.

Mō: 1)   (already)
           When used in affirmative (past) sentences.
           Mō tabemashita.   -(I) have already eaten.
           Mō kaerimashita.   -(He) has already gone back.

2) (no longer)
    When used in negative sentences
    Mō tabemasen.   -(I) will not eat any longer.
    Mō ikimasen.   -(I) will not go any longer.

Type 1: au (to meet), uru (to sell), oku (to keep), okuru (to send), yasumu (to rest, to take a holiday), sumu (to live), aruku (to walk), kiku (to ask, to listen), yomu (to read), omou (to think)

Type 2: wasureru (to forget), okureru (to be late), oshieru (to teach), mukaeru (to receive), oboeru (to remember), suteru (to throw away), kiru (to wear), kariru (to borrow), kanjiru (to feel), tariru (to suffice)

Type 3: renshū suru (to practice), annai suru (to guide), dansu suru (to dance), kopī suru (to zerox), shinpai suru (to worry), sentaku suru (to wash clothes), unten suru (to drive)

Try these:

1. Jūni-ji made _____ masu.
    benkyō suru / yomu / oshieru

2. Kinō _____ masen deshita.
    unten suru / renshū suru / yasumu

3. (fill in the blank with appropriate verb)
    Gohan o _____ masu.
    Miruku o _____ masu.
    Tegami o _____ masu.
    Shinbun o _____ masu.
    Okane o _____ masu.
    Kuruma o _____ masu.
    Fuku o _____ masu.
    Nihongo o _____ masu.

Vocabulary

araimasu .... to wash
benkyō shimasu .... to study
eiga .... movie
gurai .... about
han .... 30 minutes
hatarakimasu .... to work
ikimasu .... to go

23

kaerimasu .... to go back
kaeshimasu .... to return
kaimono................................... shopping
kakimasu.................................. to write
kara .... from
kekkon shimasu .... to marry
kimasu .... to come
korekara .... from now on
made .... till
maiasa .... every morning
maiban .... every night
mainichi .... everyday
mimasu...................................... to watch
mise .... shop
nomimasu .... to drink
okimasu..................................... to get up
ongaku .... music
oyogimasu .... to swim
pāti .... party
sake.. Japanese rice wine
shimasu .... to do
shukudai .... homework
te.. hand
tegami.. letter
yamemasu .... to quit
yasumimasu .... to have a break
zutto .... throughout

6
TE FORM OF VERBS

Lesson
1) Present continuous form
1. *Watashi wa ima tegami o kaite imasu.*
-I am writing a letter now.
2. *Watashi wa Tokyo ni sunde imasu.*
-I live in Tokyo at present.
3. *Watashi wa mō Tokyo ni sunde imasen.*
-I'm no longer living in Tokyo.
4. *Kare wa kekkon shite imasu.*
-He is married.
5. *Sensei wa nihongo no ii jisho o motte imasu.*
-My teacher has a good Japanese language dictionary.
6. *Kanojo wa piano o naratte imasu.*
-She is learning the piano.
7. *Yamada san o shitte imasu ka.*
-Do you know Mr. Yamada?

2) Making a request: Te-form of verb + 'kudasai'
1. *Tanaka san o yonde kudasai.*   -Please call Mr. Tanaka.
2. *Yukkuri hanashite kudasai.*   -Please speak slowly.
3. *Dōzo tabete kudasai.*   -Please eat.
4. *Nihongo de kaite kudasai*   -Please write in Japanese.

Making a request in negative:　　Te-form of verb +
　　　　　　　　　　　　　　　　　　　'kudasai masen ka'
(This is more polite than the above form).
1. *Tanaka san o yonde kudasai masen ka.*
　　　　　　　-Would you mind calling Mr. Tanaka?

2. *Ashita hachi-ji ni kite kudasai masenka.*
　　　　　　　-Would you mind coming at 8 o'clock tomorrow?

3. *Kare no denwabangō o oshiete kudasai masen ka.*
　　　　　　　-Would you mind telling me his telephone number?

3) Consecutive action
　　All the verbs are to be joined with Te-form with the last verb
in the appropriate form.
1. *Asa roku-ji ni okite sanpo shite asagohan o tabemasu.*
　　　　　　　-I get up at six, take a walk and have my breakfast.

2. *Yoru ku-ji ni uchi ni kaette shawā o abite bangohan o tabemasu.*
　　　　　　　-I return home at 9 o'clock, take a shower
　　　　　　　　　　　　　　　　　　and have my dinner.

Grammar:
How to make Te - form
　　Type 1 verbs

Last syllable of the verb		Te form
ku	→	ite
gu	→	ide
tsu, ru, u,	→	tte
nu, mu, bu.	→	nde
su	→	shite

e.g.)			
	kaku	→	kaite (to write)
	nugu	→	nuide (to take off)
	tatsu	→	tatte (to stand)
	noru	→	notte (to get on)
	kau	→	katte (to buy)
	shinu	→	shinde (to die)
	nomu	→	nonde (to drink)
	tobu	→	tonde (to fly)
	hanasu	→	hanashite (to speak)

Type 2 verbs
    drop 'ru' and add 'te'.

e.g.)   taberu   → tabete (to eat)

              miru   → mite (to see)

Type 3 verbs
        suru   → shite (to do)

        kuru   → kite (to come)

Try these:
1. Convert the following into present continuous form.

    Ame ga furu. (to rain)
    Onaka ga suku. (to feel hungry)
    Megane o kakeru. (to wear specs)
    Okane o harau. (to pay money)
    Hon o sagasu. (to search for a book)
    Kaisha o yasumu. (to take a day off)

2. Convert the following into 'te-kudasai' and
                            'te-kudasai masen ka' forms.

    Motto benkyō suru. (study more)
    Hon o kaesu. (return the book)
    Shigoto o tetsudau. (help in work)
    Denki o tsukeru. (switch on the light)
    Te o arau. (wash one's hands)
    Kaban o motsu. (hold the bag)

Vocabulary

abimasu	take (a shower)
asagohan	breakfast
bangohan	dinner
denwabangō	telephone number
hanashimasu	to speak
mochimasu	to have
naraimasu	to learn
sanpo shimasu	to take a walk
sensei	teacher
shawā	shower
shirimasu	to know
yobimasu	to call
yoru	night
yukkuri	slowly

7
ADVERBIAL FORM OF ADJECTIVES AND NOUNS

Lesson
1) I-adjectives - (last 'i' turns to 'ku')
+ verb (appropriate form)
1. *Raigetsu kara atsuku narimasu.*
-Next month onwards,
it will become hot.

2. *Kinō kara gasorin ga jū- en takaku narimashita.*
-Since yesterday petrol has become expensive by 10 yen.

3. *Sukoshi yasuku shite kudasai masen ka.*
-Would you kindly make it little cheaper?

4. *Atarashii uchi wa sukoshi tōku narimashita.*
-My new house is little farther.

2) Na-adjectives and nouns-add *ni* between adjective / noun and verb.
1. *(Anata wa) nihongo ga jōzu ni narimashita ne.*
-Your Japanese has become good.

2. *Minasan shizuka ni shite kudasai.*
-Everybody, please keep quiet.

3. *Ashita kara hima ni narimasu.*
-From tomorrow on I will be free.

4. *Watashi wa otōsan ni narimashita.*
-I have become a father.

5. *Watashi wa kotoshi sanjussai ni narimasu.*
-I will turn 30 this year.

Grammar:

As is obvious from the above examples, 'naru' and "suru' are the two most commonly used verbs, but some other verbs can also be used such as 'hayaku neru' (sleep early), 'yoku kangaeru' '(think well), 'osoku kuru' (come late) in case of i-adjectives and 'kirei ni saku' (bloom beautifully) 'jōzu ni hanasu' (to be eloquent) etc. in case of na-adjectives.

Try these:

Join the following using the appropriate adverbial form.

1. kurai / naru. (become dark)

2. iya / naru (get fed up)

3. benri / naru (become convenient)

4. kirei / suru (to clean)

5. taisetsu / suru (to handle carefully)

Vocabulary

gasorin	petrol
hima	free
kotoshi	this year
minasan	everybody
narimasu	become
otōsan	father
raigetsu	next month
sai (suffix)	classifier for age (see chapter 55)
sanjussai	30 years old
sukoshi	a little, bit
tōi	far

8
WANTING SOMETHING

Lesson
1) Noun +'ga hoshii desu'

1. *Watashi wa atarashii kuruma ga hoshii desu.*
   -I want a new car.

2. *Mizu ga hoshii desu.* - I want a glass of water.

3. *Kono hon wa hoshiku nai desu.* -I don't want this book.

4. *Mai hōmu ga hoshii desu ga, okane ga arimasen.*
   -I want to own a house, but I have no money.

5. *Rajikase ga hoshikatta desu ga, tēpu rekōdā shika arimasen deshita.*
   -I wanted a radio cassette tape recorder, but only a tape recorder was available.

6. *Konna mono wa hoshiku nakattan desu ga...*
   -I didn't want such a thing but...

Note: Compare the use of above form with the following forms.

2) 'masu' base (convert the verb into 'masu' form and drop 'masu') + 'tai desu'.
Note: This form is used only in case of first and second person.

1. *Watashi wa atarashii kuruma o kaitai desu.*
   -I want to buy a new car.

2. *Mizu o nomitai desu.* -I want to have water.

3. *Kono hon wa kaitaku nai desu.*
   -I don't want to buy this book.

4. *Mai hōmu o (ga) kaitai desu ga okane ga arimasen.*
   -I want to buy a house, but I have no money.

5. *Rajikase ga kaitakatta desu ga, tēpu rekōdā shika arimasen deshita.*
   -I wanted to buy a radio tape recorder, but only a tape recorder was available.

6. *Konna mono wa kaitaku nakattan desu ga...*
   -I didn't want to buy such a thing, but...

3) Noun +o 'hoshigatte imasu'
'masu' base + 'tagatte imasu' in case of verbs
Note: This form is used only in case of second and third person.

1. *Ano hito wa atarashii kuruma o hoshigatte imasu.*
   -That person wants a new car.

2. *Ano hito wa atarashii kuruma o kaitagatte imasu.*
   -That person wants to buy a new car.

3. *Kare wa ano hon o hoshigatte imasen.*
   -He doesn't want that book.

4. *Kare wa ano hon o kaitagatte imasen.*
   -He doesn't want to buy that book.

5. *Kanojo wa maihōmu o kaitagatte imasu ga, okane ga arimasen.*
   -She wants to buy a house. but has no money.

6. *Yamada san wa rajikase o hoshigatte imashita ga, tēpu rekōdā shika arimasen deshita.*
   -Mr. Yamada wanted a radio tape recorder, but only a tape recorder was available.

7. *Yamada san wa rajikase o kaitagatte imashita ga tēpu rekōdā shika arimasen deshita.*
   -Mr. Yamada wanted to buy a radio tape recorder, but only a tape recorder was available.

8. *Watashi no kodomo wa konna mono o hoshigatte imasen deshita ga...*
   -My child did not want such a thing, but...

9. *Watashi no kodomo wa konna mono o kaitagatte imasen deshita ga...*
   - My child did not want to buy such a thing, but...

4) Want someone to do something
Te form of verbs + 'hoshii desu'
1. *Nichiyōbi ni kaisha e kite hoshii desu.*
    -I want you to come to the office on Sunday.
2. *Kono shukudai o ashita made ni shite hoshii desu.*
    - I want you to do this homework by tomorrow.
3. *Anata ni itte hoshikatta desu.*
    -I wanted you to go.
4. *konna koto o shite hoshiku nakatta desu.*
    - I did not want you to do such a thing.

Grammar:
As is obvious from the lesson, 'hoshii desu' is used exclusively when wanting an object, and the other forms are used with verbs. However, besides 'hoshii' which is an i-adjective, 'tai desu' ('want' form of verbs) and 'nai desu' (negative form of want form of verbs) also follow i-adjective conjugation as they end in vowel + 'i'.

Particle 'ga' (but)- conjunction that combines two sentences.

Note: When a person does something against his/her wishes, this form is used at the end of the sentence leaving the second part of the sentence unsaid. See the last sentence of each form in the above lesson.

Particle 'shika' (only, nothing but)

Note: 'Shika' always occurs with negative form of verbs, but the meaning is positive. There is a parallel particle 'dake' which has more or less the same meaning, but the latter is used with affirmative form of verbs. Moreover 'dake' in some cases is more emphatic while 'shika' is more humble.

e.g. Watashi wa nihongo dake dekimasu.
    -I know only Japanese. (the speaker exudes confidence implying that knowing only the Japanese is good enough)
    Watashi wa nihongo shika dekimasen.
    -I know only Japanese. (the speaker feels apologetic that he knows no other language but Japanese only)

Particle 'n'
    (no)
        It is used colloquially. Any sentence in Japanese can
        be ended in this form.
  e.g.   Watashi wa *ikimasu*. →Watashi wa *ikun (ikuno)* desu.

1. Watashi wa *ikitai* desu. → Watashi wa *ikitain (ikitaino)* desu.
2. Kore wa kinō *kaimashita*. → kore wa kinō *kattan (kattano)* desu.
3. Dō *shimashita* ka. → Dō *shitan (shitano)* desu ka.

Demonstratives
    Konna - this type (kind)
    Sonna - that type (kind)
    Anna   - that type (kind)
    Donna - What type (kind)

1. Always followed by a noun and its use is as under:
   - Konna hon wa irimasen.
             -I don't need such (type of) book.
   - Donna shigoto o shite imasu ka.
             -What type of work are you doing?

2. The above set of demonstratives has yet another usage where it is followed by particle 'ni' and is mostly used in a negative sentence or at least has a negative connotation. In this case, its meaning is 'to this extent', 'to that extent,' 'to what extent'
   - Sonnani tōin (tōino) desuka - Is it that far?
   - Konnani chikakattan (chikakatta no) desu ka.
             -(I did not know that) it was so close.

'Mono' 'koto': Abstract nouns
'Mono' can replace any noun implying any physical thing and 'koto' can replace any abstract noun.

e.g.) - Konna mono wa hoshiku nai desu.
             -I don't want such a thing.
      - Watashi wa sonna koto o shimasen.
             -I don't do such a thing.

Try these:

Translate the following into English.

1. Watashi wa pen ga hoshii desu.

2. Watashi wa okii kamera ga hoshiku nai desu.

3. Kare wa hayaku kaeritagatte imasu.

4. <u>Musuko</u> wa <u>isha</u> ni nari tagatte imasu.
   (son)   (doctor)

5. (Watashi wa) mada tabetaku nai desu.

Vocabulary

kodomo	child
mai hōmu	my home
mizu	water
nichiyōbi	Sunday
okane	money
rajikase	radio cassette recorder
tēpu rekōdā	tape recorder

9
CAPABILITY FORM

1) Noun + 'ga dekiru' Used in case of possessing a special skill.
1. *Watashi wa konpyūta ga dekimasu.*
    -I can handle computer. (I know computer.)
2. *Kanojo wa ryōri ga dekimasen.*   -She can not cook.
3. *Anata wa yakyū ga dekimasu ka.*
    -Can you play baseball?

2) Verb + 'koto ga dekiru'
1. *Watashi wa odoru koto ga dekimasen.* - I can not dance.
2. *Kinō yatto denwa de tomodachi to hanasu koto ga dekimashita.*
    -Yesterday I could finally talk to my friend on phone.
3. *Mukashi ryōri o tsukuru koto ga dekimasen deshita ga, ima wa jōzu ni narimashita.*
    -Earlier I could not cook, but now I'm quite good at it.

3) Alternative capability form for *Type 1 Verbs*
Note: For type 2 and 3 verbs either 'koto ga dekiru' form or passive form can be used. (For passive form, see the relevant chapter).
Change last 'u' of the verb to 'e' and add 'masu' (exception: tsu → te)

This form always takes particle 'ga' before the verb.
| nomu | → | nomeru | → | nomemasu |
| kau | → | kaeru | → | kaemasu |

Note: Type 1 verbs, when changed to alternative capability form become type 2 verbs, as they end in 'eru'

1. *Watashi wa sake ga zenzen nomemasen. (nomu)*
    -I can not drink alcohol at all.

35

2. *Watashi wa nihongo ga sukoshi shika hanasemasen. (hanasu)*
   -I can speak only a little Japanese.

3. *Watashi wa jukkiro hashiremasu. (hashiru).*
   -I can run 10 kilometers.

4) I-adjective + capability form: change 'i' to 'kute'
+ capability form

Note: If the verb is type 1 verb, always use the alternative capability form, and in case of type 2 and 3 verbs, either use 'koto ga dekiru' or passive form.

1. *Kono kuruma wa takakute kaemasen. (kau)*
   -This car is expensive and hence I can not buy it.

2. *Kono kutsu wa chiisakute hakemasen.*
   -This shoe is small and hence I can not wear it.

3. *Kono nimotsu wa omokute motemasen.*
   -This luggage is heavy and hence I can not carry it.

4. *Kono niku wa katakute taberu koto ga dekimasen.*
   -This meat is hard, hence I can not eat it.

5) Na-adjective + capability form: add 'de' between adjective and verb + capability form.

1. *Watashi wa sake ga suki de nakanaka yameru koto ga dekimasen.*
   -I like alcohol and hence just can not give it up.

2. *Kono shigoto wa kiken de dekimasen.*
   -This job is dangerous and hence I can not do it.

Note: 'Dekimasu' is an independent verb which also means 'can do something'.

e.g.) Konpyūta ga dekimasu ka. - Can you handle computer?
   - Hai, dekimasu.   - Yes, I can.
   - Iie, dekimasen.   - No, I can't

6) Noun + capability form:

1. *Watashi wa bejitarain de niku o taberu koto ga dekimasen.*
   -I am a vegetarian and hence cannot eat meat.

Grammar:
Particle 'de': instrumental
e.g. 'te de taberu'   (eat with hand)
     'basu de iku'   (go by bus)
Particle 'to: with
     'to hanasu' (speak with)
     'to iku'   (go with)
     'to neru'   (sleep with)

Try these:
Translate the following into Japanese.
1. I can <u>drive.</u>
         (unten suru)
2. I can not <u>speak Japanese.</u>
         (Nihongo o hanasu)
3. I can play golf. (Noun + ga dekimasu)
4. I can not <u>swim.</u> (Make alternative capability form)
         (oyogu)
5. I can not <u>write</u> kanji (Make alternative capability form)
         (kaku)
6. It is <u>far</u> and hence I can not <u>go.</u>
         (toi)   (iku)
7. I <u>dislike</u> sushi hence I can not <u>eat</u> it.
     (kirai)   (taberu)

Vocabulary

hakimasu	to wear shoes / pants etc.
katai	hard
konpyūta	computer
kutsu	shoes
mukashi	earlier
nakanaka	not easily
niku	meat
nimotsu	luggage
odorimasu	to dance
omoi	heavy
ryōri	cooking
tomodachi	friend
yakyū	baseball
yatto	finally

10
SIMULTANEOUS ACTIONS

'masu' base of first verb + 'nagara'
Note: Usually the latter action is more important.

1. *Shinbun o yominagara asagohan o tabemasu.*
   -I have my breakfast while reading newspaper.
2. *Ongaku o kikinagara unten o shimasu.*
   -While driving, I listen to music.
3. *Shokuji shinagara hanashi mashō.*
   -Let's talk while having the food.
4. *Arukinagara kangaemasu.* -I think while walking.
5. *Kinō hirugohan o tabenagara shigoto no hanashi o shimashita.*
   -Yesterday we talked about business
   while having our lunch.

Try these:
Combine the following using 'nagara' form.

1. Aisukurīmu o taberu / eiga o miru
2. Tabako o suu / denwa o kakeru
3. Neru / shōsetsu o yomu
4. Kōhī o nomu / ongaku o kiku
5. Piano o hiku / uta o utau

Vocabulary

aisukurīmu .... ice cream
arukimasu .... to walk
hanashi .... talk
hikimasu .... to play (a string instrument)
hirugohan .... lunch
kakemasu .... to make (a call)
kangaemasu .... to think
nemasu .... to lie down
shigoto .... business/work
shokuji .... meal
shōsetsu .... novel
uta .... song
utaimasu .... to sing

11
EASY TO ~, DIFFICULT TO~

'masu' base of verb + 'yasui' (easy to) or 'nikui' (difficult to)
Note: Since both these expressions end in vowel + 'i', they are conjugated like i-adjective.

1. *Kono kusuri wa nomiyasui desu ka.*
   >-Is this medicine easy to take.
   - Iie amari nomiyasuku naidesu.
   >-No, it is not so easy to take.

2. *Saikin konpyūta ga kaiyasuku narimashita.*
   >-Of late, computer has become affordable.
   >(easy to purchase)

3. *Ano hito wa hanashinikui desu.*
   >-That person is a hard nut to crack. (difficult to talk to)

4. *Ano resutoran no sutēki wa tabenikukatta desu.*
   >-Steak in that restaurant was not very good.
   >(difficult to eat)

Try these:
1. Kanji wa (yomu) _____ .
   >(is difficult to read)

2. Ano hito no hanashi wa (wakaru) _____ .
   >(was difficult to understand)

3. Kono pen wa amari (kaku) _____ .
   >(is not so easy to write with)

4. Natsu wa tabemono ga (kusaru) _____ .
   >(is easy to rot)

5. Nihon-ryōri wa (taberu) ____ ga, nattō dake wa (taberu) ____ .
   >(is easy to eat)   (is difficult to eat)

Vocabulary

kanji .... Chinese character
kusuri .... medicine
natsu .... summer
nattō .... fermented beans (Japanese dish)
saikin .... recently
sutēki .... steak
tabemono .... food

12
BEFORE: Dictionary Form of Verb
+'MAE NI'
AFTER: Te Form of Verb +'KARA'

Lesson
1. *Shokuji suru mae ni te o aratte kudasai.*
   -Please wash your hands before having your meal.

2. *Te o aratte kara shokuji shite kudasai.*
   -Please have your meal after washing your hands.

3. *Denwa o kakete kara watashi no heya ni kinasai.*
   -Come to my room after having made the call.

4. *Watashi no heya ni kuru mae ni denwa o kakenasai.*
   -Make the call before coming to my room.

Grammar:
'Nasai': ordering form (used by senior to junior)
'masu' base + 'nasai'
e.g. okiru → okimasu → okinasai (get up)
     suwaru → suwarimasu → suwarinasai (sit down)
     kuru → kimasu → kinasai (come)
     benkyō suru → benkyō shimasu → benkyō shinasai
     (study)

Try these:
Make both the forms with the following pairs.

1. gyūnyū o nomu / gakkō e iku
   (drink milk)   (go to school)

2. shokuji o suru / shawā o abiru
   (have food) (take a shawer)

3. benkyō suru / asobu
   (study)   (play)

4. kusuri o nomu / neru
   (take medicine) (go to bed)

5. denki o kesu / soto ni deru
   (switch off light) (go out)

13
PLAIN FORM

So far we have focussed our attention around 'desu' 'masu' forms or the so called polite or formal style.

Since from here on we will be trying our hand at more complex sentences, we need to study the plain form. To be more precise, when an adjective or a verb comes inbetween a sentence, it needs to be put in the plain form and the adjective or verb coming at the end of the same sentence in the 'desu' or 'masu' form as heretofore. Moreover plain form is also commonly used in informal conversation as between friends, colleagues, husband and wife, parent - child, etc. However, at the same time whole text is also written in plain form such as in newspapers, magazines, thesis etc. Study the following plain forms 'desu' and verbs before proceeding further.

	masu form	dictionary form	ta-form (past)	nai-form (negative)	nakatta-form (past negative)
	desu	da	datta	dewanai	dewanakatta
Type 1 Verbs	ikimasu hanashimasu	iku hanasu	itta hanashita	ikanai hanasanai	ikanakatta hanasanakatta
Type 2 Verbs	nemasu okimasu	neru okiru	neta okita	nenai okinai	nenakatta okinakatta
Type 3 Verbs	shimasu kimasu	suru kuru	shita kita	shinai konai	shinakatta konakatta

Note: Dictionary form of 'na' adjectives and nouns is *adj./noun + da*.

Note: There can be another way of obtaining the plain form of verbs. (Type 3 verbs are exceptional and hence must be remembered by heart.)

Ta form   Change the last 'e' of te-form into 'a' (In case of type 2 verbs, simply drop 'ru' and add 'ta')

Nai form (type 1 verbs) Change the last 'u' in the dictionary form of verb into 'a' and add 'nai'. (In case of type 2 verbs simply drop 'ru' and add 'nai')

(Exceptions to type 1 verbs) tsu→ta + nai

In case of verbs ending in vowel + 'u' such as 'kau' (to buy), 'omou' (to think), warau (to laugh) etc., last 'u' changes to 'wa' + nai. 'aru' (arimasu) → 'nai (arimasen)

(Note)   'nai' form undergoes i-adjective like conjugation as it ends in vowel + 'i'. It is for this very reason that plain past form of verbs as well as 'desu' (dewanai) becomes 'katta desu'.

Nakatta form   see the Note above.

14
I THINK THAT: ~ 'TO OMOIMASU'

Appropriate plain form of verb/adjective/noun + *to omoimasu*
Note: *To omoimasu* remains the same even if the expression in
English is I don't think that ~'. In such a case, verb or
'desu' preceeding this expression is put in plain negative
form.

Lesson
1) Nouns
1. *Kore wa Yamada san no hon da to omoimasu.*
   -I think this is Mr. Yamada's book.
2. *Ashita wa yasumi dewanai to omoimasu.*
   -I don't think tomorrow is a holiday.

Note:1) Since subject is quite often omitted in Japanese, in this
   kind of sentence, it usually implies 'I think that',
   unless otherwise mentioned.
   2) Na-adjectives and nouns must always be followed by
   the appropriate form of 'da' (desu). However, in case
   of i-adjectives, 'da' is dropped altogether.

2) Adjectives
1. *Kono kamera wa atarashiku nai to omoimasu.*
   -I don't think this camera is new.
2. *Kanojo wa ashita hima da to omoimasu.*
   -I think she is free tomorrow.
3. *Watashi wa ashita hima dewanai to omoimasu.*
   -I don't think I am free tomorrow.

3) Verbs
1. *Kyō ame ga furu to omoimasu.*
   -I think (that) it will rain today.
2. *Kinō ame ga futta to omoimasu.*
   -I think it rained yesterday.

3. *Kyō ame ga furanai to omoimasu.*
   -I think it will not rain today (or)
   I don't think it will rain today.

4. *Kinō ame ga furanakatta to omoimasu.*
   -I think it did not rain yesterday.

5. *Kare wa niku o tabenai to omoimasu.*
   -I think he doesn't eat meat (or)
   I don't think he eats meat.

6. *Kare wa kinō no pātī ni konakatta to omoimasu.*
   -I think he did not come for yesterday's party.

7. *Kare wa kinō no pātī ni kite inakatta to omoimasu.*
   -I think he was not there in the party.

8. *Kare wa ima shigoto o shite inai to omoimasu.*
   -I think he is not working at present.
   or I don't think he is doing any work just now.

Try these:
Fill in the blank with the plain form.

1. Tanaka san wa ashita _____ to omoimasu.
   (yasumimasen)

2. Kono terebi wa yoku _____ to omoimasu.
   (uremasu)

3. Kare wa mada _____ to omoimasu.
   (kite imasen deshita)

4. Tokyo wa _____ to omoimasu.
   (kirei desu)

5. Ima Rondon wa _____ to omoimasu.
   (samui desu)

6. Hayashi san wa _____ to omoimasu.
   (byōki desu)

Vocabulary

ame	rain
byōki	sick
furimasu	to rain
Rondon	London
uremasu	to sell, saleable
yasumi	holiday
yoku	well

15
IT IS SAID THAT : ~'TO IIMASU'

Appropriate plain form of verb / adjective / noun + to iimasu.

Note:1) Its use is by and large same as 'to omoimasu'.
2) Also see the use of '~ to iu' in Chapter 17.

Lesson
1) Nouns
1. *Nihonjin wa shinsetsu na hitobito da to iimasu.*
   -It is said that Japanese are polite people.

2. *Ōsaka wa kinō ame datta to iimasu.*
   -It is said that it rained yesterday in Osaka.

3. *Tabako o suu no (koto) wa kenkō ni warui to iimasu.*
   -It is said that smoking is injurious to health.

2) Adjectives
1. *Nihon wa jishin ga ōi to iimasu.*
   -It is said that Japan has many earthquakes.

2. *Asoko wa sonnani shizuka dewa nai to iimasu.*
   -It is said that - that place is not so quiet.

3) Verbs
1. *Deri wa fuyu ni samuku naru to iimasu.*
   -It is said that Delhi becomes cold in winters.

2. *Nihon wa rokugatsu ni ame ga furu to iimasu.*
   -It is said that it rains in June in Japan.

Grammar:

Noun clause: no (koto) after the plain form of a verb converts the phrase (sentence) preceeding it into a noun.

e.g.) Nihon e iku no (koto) wa kantan desu.
- It is easy to go to Japan.

Nihongo o narau no (koto) wa muzukashii desu.
- It is difficult to learn Japanese.

Try these:

Translate the following into English.

1. Nihonjin wa heikin jumyō ga nagai to iimasu.

2. Kore wa nihon bunka ni tsuite ichiban ii hon da to iimasu.

3. Kare wa kinō kaisha ni konakatta to iimasu.

4. Mainichi osake o nomu no (koto) wa kenkō ni yokunai to iimasu.

Vocabulary

bunka	culture
fuyu	winter
heikin	average
hitobito	people
jumyō	life span
kenkō	health
ōi	lots of
roku gatsu	June
sonnani	not so
tsuite	about
warui	bad

16
~ IS SAYING THAT ~: 'TO ITTE IMASU'
(Says That)

Appropriate (plain) form of verbs / adjectives / noun + to itte imasu

Note: This form is commonly used in direct and indirect speech.

Lesson

1) Nouns

1. *Kare wa "Watashi wa kono daigaku no gakusei desu", to itte imasu.* (direct speech)
   -He says, "I am a student of this university."

2. *Kare wa kono daigaku no gakusei da to itte imasu.* (Indirect speech)
   -He says that he is a student of this university.

2) Adjectives

1. *Kanojo wa "Watashi wa ryōri ga tokui desu" to itte imasu.*
   -She says, "I'm good at cooking."

2. *Kanojo wa ryōri ga tokui da to itte imasu.*
   -She says that she is good at cooking.

3. *Yamada san wa "Watashi wa kyō hima de wa arimasen", to itte imashita.*
   -Mr. Yamada was saying "I am not free today."

4. *Yamada san wa kyō hima dewa nai to itte imashita.*
   -Mr. Yamada was saying that he is not free today.

5. *Sensei wa "Kono jisho wa amari yokunai desu", to itte imasu.*
   -Teacher says, "This dictionary is not so good."

6. *Sensei wa kono jisho wa amari yokanai to itte imasu.*
   -Teacher says that this dictionary is not so good.

3) Verbs

1. *Kanojo wa "Watashi wa kyō roku-ji ni kuru koto ga dekimasen", to itte imasu.*
   -She says, "I can not come at 6 o'clock today."

2. *Kanojo wa kyō roku-ji ni kuru koto ga dekinai to itte imasu.*
   -She says that she can not come at 6 o'clock today.

3. *Shujin wa "Watashi wa konban osoku narimasu", to itte imashita.*
   -My husband was saying, "I will be late (come back late) tonight."

4. *Shujin wa konban osoku naru to itte imashita.*
   - My husband was saying that he will be late tonight.

Grammar:

As obvious from above examples, direct speech is mostly used in the written language and indirect speech in the spoken language as in English.

Try these:

Change the following into indirect speech.

1. Kachō wa "Kyō no kaigi ga jūyō desu" to itte imasu.

2. Hayashi san wa "Kinō no kaigi ga omoshiroku nakkata desu" to itte imashita.

3. Kanai wa "Zehi kono eiga ga mitai desu", to itte imasu.

4. Kanojo wa "Kore wa watashi no kasa dewa arimasen"to itte imasu.

5. Kare wa "Watashi wa gyūniku o zenzen tabemasen" to itte imasu.

Vocabulary

daigaku	university
gakusei	student
gyūniku	beef
jūyō	important

51

kachō .... section chief
kanai .... my wife
konban .... tonight
kasa .... umbrella
osoi .... late
shujin .... my husband
tokui .... (be) good at
zehi .... by all means

17
CALLED, KNOWN AS~: NOUN + 'TO IU~'

Lesson
1. *Hashimoto san to iu hito o shitte imasu ka.*
   -Do you know the person called Hashimoto?
2. *'Mēdo in Japan' to iu hon o yomimashita ka.*
   -Did you read, the book entitle 'Made in Japan'?
3. *Arigatō to iu kotoba o shitte imasu ka.*
   -Do yo know the word 'Arigatō"?
4. *'Jōzu' to iu eiga o mimashita ka.*
   -Did you see the movie called 'Jaws'?
5. *'Akihabara' to iu tokoro wa doko desu ka.*
   -Where is the place called 'Akihabara'?
6. *Kinō 'yōkan' to iu nihon no okashi o tabemashita.*
   -Yesterday I had a Japanese sweet called 'Yokan'.

Try these:
Translate the following into Japanese.

1. Today a person called Mr. Suzuki came.
2. Did you climb the mountain called 'Fuji san'?
3. Where is the company called 'Sony' located?
4. The movie called 'Jaws' was very interesting.
5. Do you know the song called 'Sukiyaki?

Vocabulary

arigatō .... Thank you
kotoba .... word
noborimasu .... to climb
okashi .... snacks, sweet
tokoro.. place
totemo.. very
yama .... mountain
yōkan .... Japanese sweet

18
WHEN, AT THE TIME OF : ~ 'TOKI'

1. Noun + no toki
2. Na-adjective + na toki
3. I-adjective + toki
4. Plain form of verb + toki

Lesson
1) Nouns
1. *Kodomo no toki nihon ni sunde imashita.*
   -When I was a child, I lived in Japan.

2. *Daigakusei no toki yoku benkyō shimashita.*
   -I studied hard when I was in the university.

2) Na-adjectives
1. *Hima na toki ni nani o shimasu ka.*
   -What do you do in your free time?

2. *Taikutsu na toki terebi o mimasu.*
   -When I feel bored, I watch T.V.

3) I-adjectives
1. *Atsui toki yama e ikimasu.*
   -I go to mountains when it is hot.

2. *Wakai toki mainichi undō shimashita.*
   -When I was young, I exercised every day.

4) Verbs
1. *Osoku naru toki denwa o kudasai.*
   -Please call me when you are late.

2. *Nihon e iku toki kono tokei o kaimashita.*
   -I bought this watch when I was going to Japan.

3. *Nihon e itta toki kono tokei o kaimashita.*
    -I bought this watch when I went to Japan.

Note: Sentence 2 above implies that the watch was purchased before or on the way to Japan, and Sentence 3 implies that the watch was purchased in Japan.

Try these:
Translate the following into English.

1. Kekkon shita toki watashi wa nijūgo- sai deshita.

2. Watashi wa asagohan o taberu toki itsumo shinbun o yomimasu.

3. Nihon ni sunde ita toki, itsumo bangohan o shichi -ji ni tabemashita.

4. Hito ga ōi toki, ōkii heya de kaigi o shimasu.

5. Mendō na toki, fāsuto-fūdo o tabemasu.

6. Ame no toki, mai-kā de ikimasu.

7. Nihon e kuru toki, denwa o kudasai.

8. Nihon ni kita toki, denwa o kudasai.

Vocabulary

daigakusei	college student
fāsuto-fūdo	fast food
itsumo	always
mendō	troublesome
nijūgo-sai	25 years old
shichi-ji	7 o'clock
taikutsu	feeling bored
undō shimasu	to exercise
wakai	young

19
CAUSE / REASON: 'KARA', 'NODE'

Noun / na-adjective + 'da kara' or 'na node'
Appropriate plain form of verb + 'kara' or 'node'
I -adjective + kara or node

Note: Both have similar meaning but broadly speaking, they
have following differences.

'kara': Used in Casual / informal / spoken language or in
case of an excuse.

'node': Used in formal / written language as well as spoken
language, but mostly in case of a valid reason.

Lesson:
1) Nouns
1. *Ame na node kyō wa ikimasen.*

2. *Ame da kara kyō wa ikimasen.*
-I will not go today since it is raining.

Note: Here both the sentences have same meaning, but the
former can be said to be more formal.

3. *Byōki datta node kinō yasumimashita.*

4. *Byōki datta kara kinō yasumimashita.*
-I took off yesterday as I was ill.

Note: In case of past form of nouns 'kara' or 'node' is used
immediately after the plain past form.

2) Na-adjectives
1. *Mae no uchi wa shizuka ja (dewa)*
nakatta kara hikkoshimashita.

2. *Mae no uchi wa shizuka dewa (ja)*
   nakatta node hikkoshimashita.
   >-I moved out from the previous
   >house as it was not quiet.

Note: 'Dewa nai' or 'dewa nakkata' becomes 'ja nai' or 'ja nakatta' colloquially. Therefore in the first sentence above 'kara' and in the second sentence 'node' is more appropriate.

3) I-adjectives
1. *Ima isogashii kara (node) ato de denwa shite kudasai.*
   >-Please call later as I am busy now.

2. *Yasukatta kara futatsu kaimashita.*
   >-I bought two as it was cheap.

4) Verbs
1. *Sugu owaru kara chotto matte kudasai.*
   >-Please wait for a while as I will be through soon.

2. *Ame ga futte iru node kasa o kashite kudasaimasen ka.*
   -Would you mind lending me an umbrella as it is raining?

3. *Ano hito wa nihon ni jū-nen mo sunde ita node nihongo ga yoku wakarimasu.*
   >That person is good at Japanese as he has lived in
   >Japan for 10 long years.

5) Colloquial application of 'kara'

This form is used when the effect (result) is mentioned first and cause mentioned subsequently.

1. *Kyō wa ikimasen. Ame da kara. (desu)*

2. *Kinō yasumimashita. Byōki datta kara. (desu)*

3. *Chotto matte kudasai. Sugu owaru kara.*

Try these:
Fill in the blank with the appropriate form of 'kara' or 'node', and also translate into English.

1. Kinō tanjōbi _____, uchi ni tomodachi ga atsumari mashita.

58

2. Ashita pikunikku _____, hayaku nemashō.
3. Samui _____, mōfu o kashite kudasai.
4. Otōsan ga nete iru _____, shizuka ni shinasai.
5. Kyō wa basu de kimashita. Okane ga _____ .

(nai)

Vocabulary

ato de	later
atsumarimasu	get together
basu	bus
futatsu	two
hayaku	early
hikkoshimasu	to move out
isogashii	busy
jū-nen	10 years
kashimasu	to lend
machimasu	to wait
mōfu	blanket
owarimasu	to finish
pikunikku	picnic
sugu	soon
tanjōbi	birthday
wakarimasu	to understand

20
ALTHOUGH : 'NONI'

**Appopriate plain form of verb, adjective + 'noni',
noun, na adjective + 'na noni'**

Lesson
1. Nouns
1. *Kyō wa yasumi na noni hataraite imasu.*
   -I am working today despite being a holiday.

2. *Nichiyōbi datta noni michi ga konde imashita.*
   -Roads were crowded despite being Sunday.

2. Na-adjectives
1. *Ano hito wa uta ga heta na noni ōkii koe de utatte imasu.*
   -That person is singing loudly
   despite being a poor singer.

2. *Koko wa benri dewa (ja) nai noni takai desu.*
   -This place is expensive despite
   being not (so) convenient.

3. I-adjectives
1. *Oishii noni naze tabenain desu ka.*
   -Why are you not eating although it is tasty?

2. *Yasukatta noni kaimasen deshita.*
   -I did not buy it although it was cheap.

   - *Dōshite desu ka?*
   -Why was that?

   Iro ga ki ni iranakatta kara desu.
   -Because I did not like the colour.

4. Verbs

1. *Minna ga hataraite iru noni kare dake ga yasunde imashita.*
   -Only he was absent although everybody else was working.
2. *Okane ga nai noni kare wa rippa na uchi ni sunde imasu ne.*
   -He lives in a palatial house although he is not (so) -rich.
3. *(Watashi wa) mō hon o kaeshita noni kare wa mada kaeshite inai to itte imasu.*
   -Although I have returned his book, he says that I have not returned it.

Grammar:

Particle 'ne' : isn't it
It is a sentence-end particle where the speaker wants confirmation or concurrence from the hearer about something.
e.g) Anata wa Tanaka san desu ne.
     (If I am not mistaken), you are Mr. Tanaka.
     Anata wa osake wa dame deshita ne.
     (If I am not mistaken), you don't drink alcohol.

Try these:
Complete the following.

1. Wakai noni _____.
2. Kono kaban wa yokunai noni _____.
3. Ashita wa nichiyōbi na noni _____.
4. Kanjo wa onaka ga suite ita noni _____.
5. Kare wa genki na noni _____.

Vocabulary

iro	....	colour
kaeshimasu	....	to return
ki ni irimasu	....	to like
koe	....	voice
konde imasu	....	be crowded

61

21
INTEND TO : 'TSUMORI DESU'

Plain form of verb + 'tsumori desu'
Noun + 'no tsumori desu'
Note: There is yet another expression namely 'yotei desu' (plan
to, schedule to) which has exactly the same usage as
'tsumori desu', except the nuance.
Lesson
1.   *Watashi wa rainen nihon e iku tsumori desu.*
-I intend to go to Japan next year.

Watashi wa rainen nihon e iku yotei desu.
-I plan to go to Japan next year.

2.   *Ashita pāti ni iku tsumori desu ka.*
-Do you intend to go to tomorrow's party?
- *Hai, iku tsumori desu.*
-Yes, I intend to.
- *Iie, ikanai tsumori desu.*
-No, I don't intend to.

3.   *Anna hito to mō hanasanai tsumori desu.*
- I don't intend to talk to such a person ever again.

4.   *Kare ni atte setsumei suru tsumori desu.*
-I intend to meet him and explain (everything).

5.   *Kondo no yasumi ni nani o suru tsumori desu ka.*
-What do you intend to do during
the coming holiday (s)?

6.   *Watashi wa iku tsumori deshita ga isogashiku narimashita.*
-I intended to go, but got busy.

63

7. *Watashi wa jōdan no tsumori de itta noni, kare wa okori-mashita.*

    -Although I said it jokingly (with the intention of a joke), but he got angry.

8. *Asobi no tsumori de nihongo o hajimemashita ga, ima wa ninongo no sensei ni narimashita.*

    - Although I started learning Japanese as a pastime, but now I am teaching it.

Try these:
Translate the following into Japanese.

1. I intend to give up my present job.
2. I don't intend to live here for <u>long</u>. (nagai)
3. After <u>retirement</u>, I intend to live in a small city. (teinen taishoku suru)
4. I don't intend to get married <u>all my life</u>. (isshō)

Vocabulary

asobi	pastime
hajimemasu	to start
iimasu	to say
jōdan	joke
kondo	next time
machi	city
mō~nai	not anymore
okorimasu	to get angry
rainen	next year
setsumei shimasu	to explain
yamemasu	to give up

22
MAY, MIGHT: 'KAMO SHIREMASEN'

Appropriate plain form of verbs + 'kamo shiremasen'
I-adjectives + 'kamo shiremasen'
'Da' base of nouns / Na-adjectives + 'kamo shiremasen'

Lesson (1)

1. *Kore ga kare no kasa kamo shiremasen.*
   -This might be his umbrella.

2. *Asoko wa koko yori shizuka kamo shiremasen.*
   -That place might be quieter (than this place).

3. *Watashi mo ashita eiga ni ikeru kamo shiremasen.*
   -I might be able to come for the movie.

4. *Kare wa mō kite iru kamo shiremasen.*
   -He might have already come.

5. *Nihon wa ima samui kamo shiremasen.*
   -Japan may be cold now.

Definitely, surely: ~ ni chigai arimasen
must have (be)

Note: This expression has exactly similar usage as 'kamo shiremasen' except that the speaker is sure about his statement in this case whereas there is some amount of doubt or probablity in case of 'kamo shiremasen'

Compare the following sentences with those in the lesson above.

Lesson (2)

1. *Kore wa kare no kasa ni chigai arimasen.*
   -This umbrella is definitely his.

2. *Asoko wa koko yori shizuka ni chigai arimasen.*
   -That place is definitely quiter than this.

3. *Kare wa mō kite iru ni chigai arimasen.*
   -He must have already come.

4. *Nihon wa ima samui ni chigai arimasen.*
   -Japan must be cold now.

Note: '~ni chigai arimasen' can not be used in case of sentence 3 in lesson (1) as the speaker is not sure about his going for the movie. Even if the speaker is sure he would say, *Watashi mo ashita eiga ni ikimasu.* If he wishes to emphasize, then he can use 'kanarazu' (without fail).

It is expected that ~
Should, ought to ~ } **hazu desu**
I'm fairly certain that ~
Appropriate form of verb / 'I' adjective + hazu desu.
 Na-adjective+'na' hazu desu. (in case of plain affirmative)
 Na-adjective+ 'datta' hazu desu. (in case of plain past)
 noun + 'no' hazu desu.

* Compare the following sentences with those in the previous two lessons.

Lesson (3)

1. *Kore ga kare no kasa no hazu desu.*
   -I'm fairly certain that it is his umbrella.

2. *Asoko wa koko yori shizuka na hazu desu.*
   -That place ought to be quieter than this place.

3. *Watashi wa ashita eiga ni ikeru hazu desu.*
   -I should be able to come for the movie tomorrow.

4. *Kare wa mō kite iru hazu desu.*
   -He must have already come.

5. *Nihon wa ima samui hazu desu.*
   -Japan is likely to be cold.

6. *Kare wa ashita shiken da kara, pāti ni kuru hazu ga arimasen (nai desu).*

> - Since he has an exam tomorrow, I am fairly certain that he will not come for the party.

7. *kono kisetsu ni yuki ga furu hazu ga arimasen* (colloquially *'nai'*).

> It is unlikely to snow in this season.

Try these:

Fill in the blank with appropriate form of 'kamo shiremasen' '~ni chigai arimasen' or 'hazu desu' (ga arimasen) and note the change in meaning.

1. Ano machi wa kirei _____.

2. Kare wa mada kaisha ni iru _____.

3. Kore wa imōto no kaban _____.

4. Ano apāto wa hirokute akarui _____.

5. Ano uchi wa mada aite iru _____.

Vocabulary

aite imasu	vacant
apāto	apartment
imōto	younger sister
kisetsu	season
shiken	exam
yuki	snow

23
JUST ABOUT TO : '~TOKORO DESU'

Lesson (1) Dictionary form of verb + 'tokoro desu'

1. *Ima kara kaisha e iku tokoro desu.*
   -I'm just about to go to office.

2. *Ima gohan o taberu tokoro desu.*
   -I'm just about to have my meal.

3. *Kore kara nihongo no benkyō o hajimeru tokoro desu.*
   -I'm just about to study Japanese language.

JUST HAD, JUST FINISHED

Lesson (2) Past form of verb + '~tokoro desu'

1. *Ima kōcha o nonda tokoro desu.*
   -I have just had tea.

2. *Tatta ima okita tokoro desu.*
   -I have just got up.

3. *Hayashi san wa ima kita tokoro desu.*
   -Mr. Hayashi has just come.

In the midst of

Lesson (3) Present continuous form + 'tokoro desu : is ~ing

1. *Ima kōcha o nonde iru tokoro desu.*
   -I'm just now having tea.

2. *Chōdo ima gohan o tabete iru tokoro desu.*
   -I'm just having my meal.

3. *Ima kare ni denwa o kakete iru tokoro desu.*
   -I'm just making a call to him.

Lesson (4) Past continuous form + 'tokoro desu': was ~ ing

1. *Ima anata ni denwa o kakete ita tokoro desu.*
   -I was just making a call to you.
2. *Chōdo ima anata no koto o kangaete ita tokoro desu. 'Uwasa o sureba kage' desu ne.*
   -I was just thinking about you.
   'Remember the devil...', isn't it?
3. *Watashi mo ima sono bangumi o mite ita tokoro desu.*
   -I was also just watching that programme.

Lesson (5) Dictionary form of verb + 'tokoro deshita': had almost, was just about

Note: This form is used when the speaker narrowly escaped a mishap.

1. *Ima korobu tokoro deshita.*
   -I almost had a fall just now.
2. *Kyō pūru de oboreru tokoro deshita.*
   -I almost drowned at the pool today.
3. *Sakki konpyūta o tsukue kara otosu tokoro deshita.*
   -I almost dropped the computer from the table a little while ago.

Grammar:

Indirect object particle 'ni'

e.g) 1. Tomodachi ni tegami o kakimasu.
   -I write a letter to my friend.

2. Kono hon o kare ni watashite kudasai.
   -Please hand this book over to him.

Try these:

Translate the following into English.

1. (Watashi wa) eiga o mi ni iku tokoro desu.
2. Tatta ima gohan o tabeta tokoro desu.
3. Ima sono repōto o kaite iru tokoro desu.
4. Ima kare to denwa de hanashite ita tokoro desu.
5. Kyō densha no jiko de shinu tokoro deshita.

Vocabulary

bangumi	programme
chōdo ima	just now (doing)
densha	train
jiko	accident
korobimasu	to fall down
oboremasu	to drown
otoshimasu	to drop
pūru	pool
repōto	report
shinimasu	to die
tatta ima	just now (finished)

24
HAVE MADE IT A POINT,
HAVE DECIDED TO

Appropriate plain form of
verb + ~ koto ni shite imasu

Lesson (1)

1. *Watashi wa maiasa sanpo suru koto ni shite imasu.*
   > -I have made it a point (practice)
   > to go for a walk every morning.

2. *Watashi wa hiru kara osake o nomanai koto ni shite imasu.*
   > -I have made it a point not to drink
   > in the daytime. (at lunch time)

3. *Watashi wa mainichi ichi-jikan nihongo o benkyō suru koto ni shite imasu.*
   > -I have made it a point to study
   > Japanese for one hour everyday.

4. *Watashi wa anna hito ni nidoto awanai koto ni shite imasu.*
   > -I have decided not to meet such a person again.

5. *Wakai toki, watashi wa mainichi go-kiro aruku koto ni shite imashita.*
   > -When young, I had made it a practice
   > to walk 5 kilometers a day.

6. *Watashi wa itsumo hayaku neru koto ni shite imashita ga, konogoro isogashikute hayaku neru koto ga dekimasen.*
   > -I had made it a point to always sleep early,
   > but these days I can not do it as I am busy.

Lesson (2) Have decided to, Have made up my mind
Appropriate plain form of verb + 'koto ni shimashita'

1. *Watashi mo pikunikku ni iku koto ni shimashita.*
   > -I have also made up my mind to go on picnic.

2. *Watashi wa pikunikku ni ikanai koto ni shimashita.*
    -I have decided not to go on picnic.

3. *Watashi wa kaisha o yameru koto ni shimashita.*
    -I have decided to quit the company.

4. *Watashi wa tabako o suwanai koto ni shimashita.*
    -I have decided not to smoke.

5. *Watashi wa kare to kekkon suru koto ni shimashita.*
    -I have decided to marry him.

Try these:
Translate the following into Japanese.

1. I have made it a point to get up by 6 o'clock.

2. I have made it a point to eat (my) breakfast <u>properly</u>.
    (shikkari)

3. I have made it a point not to have <u>tap water</u> when travelling. (namamizu)

4. I had made it a point to have <u>a glass of</u> milk everyday when I was a child. (ippai)

5. I had made it a point to eat a lot of fruits when I was sick.

6. I have decided to go to mountains during the summer vacation.

7. I have decided not to go to office by car.

Vocabulary

go-kiro	5 kilometers
hiru	noon
ichi-jikan	for 1 hour
konogoro	these days
kudamono	fruit
natsu yasumi	summer vacation
nidoto	never
ryokō shimasu	to travel
takusan	a lot of

25
HAS BEEN DECIDED: 'KOTO NI NARIMASHITA'

Appropriate plain form of
verb + 'koto ni narimashita'

Lesson (1)

1. *Kare wa tenkin suru koto ni narimashita.*
   -He is being transfered. (it has been decided to transfer him)

2. *Kyō kara kaisha de tabako ga suenai koto ni narimashita.*
   -Starting today, it has been decided to ban smoking in the office. (one can not smoke in the office)

3. *Kore kara daigaku de maitsuki shiken o suru koto ni narimashita.*
   -It has been decided to have an exam every month in the university.

Lesson (2)

Has been arranged, supposed to: koto ni natte imasu.

Appropriate plain form of verb + 'koto ni natte imasu'

1. *Ashita jūichi-ji ni shachō to au koto ni natte imasu.*
   -Tomorrow I'm supposed to meet the president of the company.

2. *Kyō no bangohan wa resutoran de taberu koto ni natte imasu.*
   -Today we are supposed to have our dinner at a restaurant.

3. *Watashi wa rainen kara kono daigaku de nihongo o oshieru koto ni natte imasu.*
   -I am supposed to teach Japanese in this university from next year.

Try these:

Change the following into 'koto ni narimashita' form.

1. Raigetsu kara furui ichimanen-satsu ga tsukaemasen.
2. Kaisha ni taimu kādo no kikai o iremasu.
3. Uchi no kaisha dewa minna ga onaji seifuku o kimasu.
4. Nihon de unten suru toki, keitai denwa ga tsukaemasen.
5. Watashi no kaisha wa isshūkan <u>ijō</u> yasumemasen.
   (more than)

Vocabulary

ichimanen satsu...	10,000 yen note
iremasu	to install
isshūkan	for a week
keitai denwa	cellular phone
kikai	machine
maitsuki	every month
onaji	same
oshiemasu	to teach
seifuku	uniform
shachō	president of the company
taimu kādo	time card
tenkin shimasu	to be transferred
tsukaimasu	to use
uchi no	our

26
SOMETIMES : 'KOTO GA ARIMASU'

Plain form of verb + 'koto ga arimasu'
Lesson (1)
1. *Watashi wa nihon ryōri o taberu koto ga arimasu'.*
                                -I sometimes eat Japanese food.
2. *Anata wa hitoride osake o nomu koto ga arimasu ka.*
                                -Do you sometimes drink (liquor) alone?
   Iie, hotondo (metta ni) nomimasen.
                                -No. I hardly ever drink alone.
3. *Yamada san no uchi ni iku koto ga arimasu ka.*
                                -Do you sometimes go to Mr. Yamada's house?
   Hai, tokidoki ikimasu.
                                -Yes, I go sometimes.
4. *Suzuki san wa anata no uchi ni kuru koto ga arimasu ka.*
                                -Does Mr. Suzuki come to your house sometimes?
   Iie, metta ni (hotondo) kimasen.
                                -No, he hardly ever comes.
5. *Tokidoki kuruma de kaisha ni iku koto ga arimasu ka.*
                                -Do you sometimes go to office by car?
   Hai, tokidoki ikimasu.
                                -Yes, I sometimes go by car.
6. *Anata wa kaji o tetsudau koto ga arimasu ka.*
                                -Do you sometimes help (your wife)
                                          in household work?
   Hai, yoku tetsudai masu.
                                -Yes. I often lend a helping hand.

Grammar:
1. Adverb 'tokidoki' also means 'sometimes' and can be used independently as in some of the examples in the lesson above. However, it can also be used as a pair with 'koto ga arimasu'.

2. As explained earlier 'koto' is an abstract noun. Therefore in this pattern sometimes it can be replaced with another noun. It is mostly used when a person does reverse of his normal routine, and the form used is negative form of verb + (usually) 'hi ga arimasu'.

e.g.) Kuruma de kaisha ni ikanai hi ga arimasu ka.
> Are there days when you don't use your car for going to office?

Sake o nomanai hi ga arimasu ka.
> Are there days when you don't drink?

Adverb 'Metta ni' (rarely): metta ni always takes negative form at the end.

e.g.), Watashi wa metta ni eiga o mimasen.
> I rarely watch any movie.

Watashi wa metta ni niku o tabemasen.
> I rarely eat meat.

Try these:
Translate the following into Japanese.

1. Do you sometimes play golf? (gorufu o suru)
2. Do you sometimes wash clothes? (sentaku suru)
3. Do you sometimes read Japanese newspaper?
4. Do you sometimes go for a walk? (sanpo suru)

Vocabulary

hitoride	by oneself
kaji	household work
tetsudaimasu	to help
yoku	often

27
EXPERIENCE

**Have the experience of, ever (been)
past form of verb + 'koto ga arimasu'**

Lesson

1. *Anata wa sushi o tabeta koto ga arimasu ka.*
   -Have you ever tried (eaten) sushi?
   -Hai, ichido dake (tabeta koto ga) arimasu.
   -Yes. I have tried only once.

2. *Anata wa nihon e itta koto ga arimasu ka.*
   -Have you been to Japan?

3. *(Anata wa) Tājimahāru o mita koto ga arimasu ka.*
   -Have you ever seen Taj Mahal?

4. *Nihon no sentō ni itta koto ga arimasu ka.*
   -Have you ever been to Japanese public bath?

Try these:
Convert the following into 'koto ga arimasu' form.

1. Fuji san ni noboru. (climb Mt. Fuji)
2. Kono shōsetsu o yomu. (read this novel)
3. Nihonshu o nomu. (drink Japanese sake)
4. Hikōki ni noru. (travel by air)
5. Kuruma o unten suru. (drive a car)

Vocabulary

ichido	once
sentō	Japanese public bath
sushi	raw fish

28
NON-CONSECUTIVE ACTION

Sometimes ~ and sometimes
'ta' base of first verb + 'tari', 'ta' base of second verb + 'tari' + 'shimasu'.

Note: Verbs ending in 'mu', 'bu' become 'dari'
e.g. nomu →nondari, yobu → yondari

Lesson (1)

1. *Watashi wa nichiyōbi ni sōji shitari, sentaku shitari shimasu.*
   -On Sundays, (sometimes) I clean my house and (at other times) wash clothes etc..

2. *Kaisha de repōto o kaitari, okyaku san ni attari shimasu.*
   -In the office, (sometimes) I write reports and (at other times) attend to guests.

3. *Kono mae no doyōbi ni eiga ni ittari, kaimono shitari shimashita.*
   -Last Saturday I watched movie and went shopping etc.

4. *Kino pāti de utattari, odottari shimashita.*
   -Yesterday in the party, we sang songs and danced.

Lesson (2)
Sometimes I do, ~ sometimes I don't
'Ta' base of first verb + 'tari' + 'nai' base of second verb + nakattari' + 'shimasu'.

1. *Anata wa mainichi sake o nomimasu ka.*
   -Do you drink everyday?
   -Iie, nondari, nomanakattari shimasu.
   -No, sometimes I drink, sometimes I don't.

2. *Anata wa mainichi undō shimasu ka.*
   -Do you exercise everyday?

-Iie, (undō) shitari shinakattari shimasu.
> -No, sometimes I do, sometimes I don't.

3. *(Anata ga) gakusei no toki mainichi arubaito o shimashita ka.*
> -Did you work as a part-timer everyday
> when you were a student?

-Iie, (arubaito o) shitari shinakattari shimashita.
> -No, sometimes I worked, sometimes I didn't.

Grammar: ~tari~tari form is used for at least 2 non-consecutive actions but can also be used for inexhaustible number of actions. All the verbs are converted to 'tari' form and 'suru' is added after the last verb and is conjugated appropriately. Compare this form with 'the consecutive action' (Chapter 6,Lesson 3).

Try these:
Convert the following sets of verbs into 'tari, ~ tari' form.

1. ryōri o tsukuru / terebi o miru
   (cook food)   (watch television)

2. (kurasu de) bun o tsukuru / kaiwa o suru
          (make sentences)   (converse)

3. tomodachi no uchi e iku / tomodachi o uchi ni yobu
   (go to friend's place)   (call a friend over)

4. asagohan o taberu / tabenai
   (eat breakfast)   (do not eat)

5. kurasu ni deru / denai
   (attend class)   (do not attend)

Vocabulary

arubaito	part-time job
kono mae no	last, previous
okyaku san	guest
sentaku shimasu	to wash clothes
sōji shimasu	to clean a place

29
A PARTICULAR CONDITION
REMAINING UNALTERED : ~ 'MAMA'

Lesson (1)
Past form ('ta' form) of verb + 'mama' (as it is)

1. *Kinō terebi o tsuketa mama nete shimaimashita.*
   -Yesterday I fell asleep with the T.V. on.
2. *Nihon dewa kutsu o haita mama uchi ni haitte wa ikemasen.*
   -One is not supposed to enter a Japanese house with shoes on.
3. *Kinō shatsu no poketto ni okane o ireta mama sentaku shite shimaimashita.*
   -Yesterday (by mistake) I washed my shirt with money in the pocket.
4. *Kare wa nihon e itta mama kaerimasen deshita.*
   -He went to Japan never to return again.
5. *Suwatta mama meishi o hito ni ageru no wa shitsurei desu.*
   -It is impolite to give one's business card to someone while sitting.

Lesson (2) noun + 'no mama'
1. *Sashimi wa nama no mama tabemasu.*
   -Sashimi is eaten in raw form (as it is).
2. *Nihon dewa kutsu no mama uchi ni haitte wa ikemasen.*
   -One is not supposed to enter a Japanese house with shoes on.
3. *Dōshite heya ga kinō no mama ni natte irun desu ka.*
   -Why the room has not been cleaned?
   (since yesterday's party / meeting).
   (Why the room is in the same condition as yesterday?)

4. *Kono machi wa mukashi no mama desu.*

> -This city continues to be as it was in the ancient times.

Note: Yet another usage of 'mama' is with 'kono' or 'sono'.

e.g.)   Kono okashi wa kono mama tabemasu.

> -This sweet is eaten as it is.

Sono mama ni shite oite kadasai.

> -Please leave it as it is.

Try these:

Make sentences with following verbs using 'mama' form.

1. tokei o hameru / ofuro ni hairu
   (wear watch)   (take bath)

2. denki o tsukeru / nete shimau
   (put on light)   (fall asleep)

3. tebukuro o suru / akushu shite wa ikemasen
   (wear gloves)   (should not shake hands)

4. asobi ni iku / renraku ga nai.
   (go for outing)   (no contact)

Vocabulary

agemasu	to give
dōshite	why
hairimasu	to enter
iremasu	to put
meishi	business card
mukashi	ancient times
nama	raw
poketto	pocket
shatsu	shirt
shitsurei	impolite
suwarimasu	to sit
tsukemasu	to switch on

30
ADVICE

Lesson (1) Advise in affirmative
Plain past form of verb + 'hō ga ii desu' (had better)

1. *Byōin e itta hō ga ii desu.*
   -You had better go to hospital.

2. *Shiken ga chikai kara benkyō shita hō ga ii desu.*
   -Since the exam is approaching, you had better study.

3. *Kaigi ga jū-ji dakara ima sugu deta hō ga ii desu.*
   -Since the meeting is at 10 o'clock, you had better leave now itself.

4. *Mō sukoshi hito no koto mo kangaeta hō ga ii desu.*
   -You had better put yourself in other person's position.

5. *Sonna koto wasureta hō ga ii desu yo.*
   -You had better forget about it. (such unpleasant experience)

6. *Shibaraku yasunda hō ga ii desu yo.*
   -You had better take a break from work for a while.

Lesson (2) Advise in negative
Plain negative + hō ga ii desu (had better not)

1. *Yoru hitori de soto ni ikanai hō ga ii desu.*
   -You had better not go out alone at night.

2. *Konna ni tabako o suwanai hō ga ii desu.*
   -You had better not smoke so much.

3. *Shokuji no mae ni kono kusuri o nomanai hō ga ii desu.*
   -You had better not take this medicine before meals.

4. *Namamizu o nomanai hō ga ii desu.*
                         -You had better not drink tap water.

Try these:
Fill in the blank with affirmative or negative advice form.

At the hospital
Patient: Sumimasen. onaka ga itain desu ga...
Doctor: (After examining)
        Sō desu ne. Netsu mo sukoshi arimasu ne.
        Kyō wa kaisha o _____.
                        (yasumu)

        Sorekara, amari gohan o _____. Dekiru dake
        okayu o_____ .   (taberu)
                (taberu)

        Furūtsu jūsu mo _____.
           (fruit juice)   (nomu)
Patient: Kusuri wa?
Doctor: Futsuka kan dake _____.
         (for 2 days)   (nomu)

        Sore kara osake wa shibaraku _____.
                                        (nomu)
        Netsu ga aru aida wa ofuro nimo
        _____ . Jā, mikka go ni mō ichido kite kudasai.
        (hairu)   (3 days later)

Patient: Dōmo arigatō gozaimashia.

Vocabulary

aida	while, during
byōin	hospital
dekiru dake	as much (many) as possible
demasu	to come out
hitori	alone
itai	pain
mo	also
mō	more

mō ichido .... once more
netsu .... fever
ofuro....................................... bath
okayu .... porridge
onaka .... stomach
shibaraku .... for a while
sorekara .... then
sugu .... immediately
wasuremasu .... to forget

31
OBLIGATION

'Nai' base of verb+'nakereba narimasen', 'nakereba ikemasen' :must, should

Note: Both these expressions have exactly the same meaning and are interchangeable. However the former is more commonly used.

Lesson

1. *Mō sorosoro kaeranakereba narimasen / ikemasen.*
    -I must go back now.

2. *Ashita shucchō dakara, hayaku nenakereba narimasen.*
    -I must go to bed early as I have a business trip tomorrow.

3. *Unten suru toki wa shito beruto o shinakereba narimasen.*
    -One must fasten the seat belt when driving.

4. *Pikunikku ni ikitai hito wa kyō okane o harawanakereba narimasen.*
    -Those who want to go on picnic must pay the money today.

5. *Dōshite watashi ga ikanakereba narimasen ka.*
    -Why is it that only I have to go?

Note: Colloquially 'nakereba narimasen' becomes 'nakucha'. It is mostly used for oneself but can be used for intimate friends or by a senior for junior.

e.g. 1. Mō sorosoro kaeranakucha.
2. Ashita shucchō da kara, hayaku nenakucha.
3. Ashita wa shiken dakara ganbaranakucha.
    -You must study hard for tomorrow's exam.
    (as you have an exam tomorrow)

85

Try these:

Change the following sentences into 'nakereba narimasen' form.

1. Shigoto ga ōi node doyōbi ni kaisha e kuru.
2. Mō jū-ji dakara sorosoro kaeru.
3. Kono repōto o ashita made ni dasu.
4. Kaisha ga tōi kara uchi o hayaku deru.
5. Atarashii ie o kau tame ni rōn o kariru.

(loan)

Vocabulary

dashimasu	to submit
doyōbi	Saturday
haraimasu	to pay
ie	house
jū-ji	10 o'clock
karimasu	to borrow
ōi	much
shimemasu	to fasten
shito beruto	seat belt
shucchō	business trip
sorosoro	soon
tame ni	for

32
PERMISSION IN NEGATIVE

'nai' base of verb + 'naku temo ii desu': need not

Lesson

1. *Ashita konakutemo ii desu.*

   -You need not come tomorrow.

2. *Watashi wa konban hayaku kaeranaku temo ii desu.*

   -I don't need to go home early tonight.

3. *Kare wa kūkō kara jibun de kuru kara, mukae ni ikanaku temo ii desu.*

   -You need not receive him at the airport as he will manage himself.

4. *Muri shite tabenakutemo ii desu.*

   -You need not eat if you don't like. (Please don't force yourself)

5. *Mō kusuri o nomanakutemo ii desu.*

   -You need not take medicine any longer.

6. *Ima okane o harawanakutemo ii desu ka.*

   -Is it O.K. if I don't pay now.

Try these:
Convert the following into 'nakutemo ii desu', and also translate it into English.

1. Zenbu oboeru.
2. Kono hon o kaesu.
3. Okane o harau.
4. Kaisha ni modoru.

5. <u>Wazawaza</u> koko e kuru.
   (all the way)
6. <u>Shinpai suru.</u>
   (worry)

Vocabulary

jibun de	by oneself
modorimasu	to return
mukaemasu	to receive
muri shimasu	to force oneself
oboemasu	to remember
zenbu	all, everything

33
REQUEST IN NEGATIVE

'nai' base of verb + 'naide kudasai': Please don't ~

Lesson

1. *Enpitsu de kakanaide kudasai.*
    > -Please don't write with pencil.

2. *Konna koto nido to shinaide kudasai.*
    > -Please don't do such a thing again.

3. *Kaigishitsu de tabako o suwanaide kudasai.*
    > -Please don't smoke in the meeting room.

4. *Okane no mudazukai o shinaide kudasai.*
    > -Please don't waste money.

5. *Jugyōchū hanasanaide kudasai.*
    > -Please don't talk in the class.

6. *Amari muri shinaide kudasai.*
    > -Please don't stretch yourself too far.

Try these:
Translate the following into English.

1. Osake o nonde kuruma o unten shinaide kudasai.

2. Sonna ni okoranaide kudasai.
    (okoru: get angry)

3. Ashita dake wa yasumanaide kudasai.

4. Kaji no toki erebētā o tsukawanaide kudasai.
    (fire)　　　(elevator)　(tsukau)

5. Mada denki o kesanaide kadasai.

Vocabulary

jugyōchū .... during the class
kaigishitsu .... meeting room
mudazukai o shimasu .... to waste

34
PERMISSION

'te' base of verb + 'temo ii desu' : may
'temo kamaimasen'
'temo daijōbu desu'

Lesson (1)
Note: All these expressions have exactly the same meaning
and are interchangeable. However the first one is more
commonly used.

1. *Kyō wa hayaku kaettemo ii desu /kamaimasen.*
   -You may go back early today.

2. *Kono hon o ichinichi karitemo ii desu ka.*
   -May I borrow this book for a day?

3. *Denwa o karitemo ii desu ka.*
   -May I use your phone?

4. *Kono pēji no kopi o tottemo ii desu ka.*
   -May I take a copy of this page?

Try these I:
Translate the following into Japanese.
   1. May I smoke?
   2. May I switch on the T.V.?
   3. May I come late tomorrow?
   4. May I ask a question?
   5. May I <u>take</u> this magazine home?
      (motte iku)

Lesson (2) Noun   + 'demo ii desu'
   Na-adjective + kutemo ii desu.
   Nai-base of i-adjective + kutemo ii desu

Note: Plain negative form of verbs, nouns, na-adjectives is also conjugated like i-adjective. For verbs see Chapter 32 on "Permission in negative". In case of i-adjective it becomes — *nakutemo ii desu* and in case of na-adjective it becomes *dewanakutemo ii desu*.

1. *Bōru pen ga nai node enpitsu demo ii desu ka.*
   -Since I don't have a ball-pen, will a pencil do?

   Hai, enpitsu demo kamaimasen.
   -Yes, I don't mind (even a pencil).

2.A: *Apāto no ken desu ga, jukkai demo ii desu ka.*
   -It is about the apartment (you are looking for), will 10th floor do?

   B: *Zenzen kamaimasen.*
   -I don't mind at all.

   A: *Mawari ga nigiyaka demo ii desu ka.*
   -Is it O.K. if the surroundings are little noisy?

   B: *Shikata ga arimasen ne.*
   -Can't help it.

   A: *Sorekara basho ga benri dakara yachin wa chotto takakutemo ii desu ka.*
   -One more thing. Since it is conveniently located, do you mind if the rent is slightly higher?

   B: *Tonikaku ichido misete kudasai masen ka.*
   -In any case, could you show me the place once?

   A: *Soreto mō hitotsu, ribingu rūmu ga amari hiroku nakutemo daijōbu desu ka.*
   -There is one more thing. Is it O.K. if the living room is not so spacious?

Try these II:
Convert the following into 'temo/demo ii desu' form.

1. chiisai jisho
2. amari <u>hiete</u> inai bīru
   (chilled)   •

3. basho ga fuben
4. eki kara tōi
5. apāto ga amari hiroku nai
6. mawari ga kirei dewa nai

Vocabulary

bīru	beer
basho	place
ichinichi	for a day
jukkai	10th floor
ken	matter
kopī o torimasu	to take a copy
mō hitotsu	one more thing
mawari	surroundings
misemasu	to show
nigiyaka	noisy, lively
pēji	page
ribingu rūmu	living room
shikata ga arimasen	can't help it
shitsumon shimasu	to ask a question
tonikaku	in any case, anyway
yachin	house rent

35
PROHIBITION

'te' form of verb + ~'wa ikemasen' $\Big\}$ should not,
                    ~ 'wa dame desu'   must not

Lesson

1. *Koko de tabako o sutte wa ikemasen / dame desu.*
    -You should not smoke here.

2. *Hito no tegami o yonde wa ikemasen.*
    -You should not read someone's letter.

3. *Jūhassai ika no hito wa unten shite wa ikemasen.*
    -People below 18 years of age must not drive.

4. *Koko ni gomi o sutete wa ikemasen.*
    -No garbage dumping here.

5. *Koko ni haitte wa ikemasen.*
    -Keep away. (Don't enter)

6. *Hinzū kyōto wa gyūniku o tabete wa ikemasen ka. (ikenain desuka)*
    -Is it true that Hindus are not supposed to eat beef? (must not eat beef)

Note: Both 'te wa ikemasen' and 'te wa dame desu' have same meaning but the latter is more informal, and colloquially it becomes 'cha (ja) dame desu/ (da) yo'.

e.g.) Koko de tabako o succha dame dayo.
       Hito no tegami o yonja dame yo.
       Koko ni haiccha dame dayo.

Try these:
Convert the following into 'tewa ikemasen' form.

1. Ima terebi o miru.
2. Koko ni <u>chūsha</u> o suru.
   (park)
3. Kūkō de shashin o toru.
4. Unten shinagara keitai denwa o tsukau.
5. Hitori de zenbu taberu.

Vocabulary

gomi	garbage
Hinzū kyōto	Hindus
ika	below
jūhassai	18 years old
shashin	photo
sutemasu	to throw
torimasu	to take (photos)

36
WITHOUT

Lesson (1) 'nai' base of verb + 'nai de ~'
                               'zu ni ~' } **: without doing~**

Note: Both 'nai de' and 'zuni' have same meaning but the former is more commonly used colloquially.

1. *Kyō wa asagohan o tabenaide kimashita.*
                         (tabezu ni)
                            -I came without (eating) breakfast.

2. *Nōto o minaide kotaete kudasai.*
             (mizu ni)
                  -Please answer without seeing your notebook.

3. *Yūbe ofuro ni hairanaide nemashita.*
               (hairazu ni)
                -Last night I went to sleep without taking bath.

4. *Konpyūta o minaide kawanai hō ga ii desu.*
                         -You had better not purchase the computer without seeing it.

5. *Setsumeisho o yomanaide kono kikai o tsukawanaide kudasai.*
-Please don't use this machine without reading the manual.

Note: In case of noun 'nashi' is used to mean 'without'.

e.g.) Kyō wa asagohan nashi de kimashita.
Okane nashide seikatsu dekimasen.
(One cannot live without money)

Lesson (2) 'nai' base of verb + ~'nai de hoshii desu'
: don't want you to~

Note: Also see Chapter 8 on 'hoshii'.

1.   *Hoka no hito ni iwanaide hoshiin desu ga.*
                    -I do not want you to tell this to others.

2.   *Ima yasunde iru kara, denki o tsukenaide hoshii desu.*
                    -Since I am resting, I don't want
                    you to switch on the light.

3.   *Watashi no soba de tabako o suwanaide hoshii desu.*
                    -I don't want you to smoke close to me.

4.   *Minna nete imasu kara shizuka ni shite hoshii desu.*
                    -Since everybody is a sleep, I want you to be quiet.

5.   *Yoru osoku denwa o kakenaide hoshii desu.*
                    -I don't want any calls late in the evening.

Try these:
Translate the following into Japanese.

1.   I don't want you to go back as yet.
2.   I went to meet him without (taking) an appointment.
3.   I don't want you to wait for me.
4.   I don't want him to come with me.
5.   <u>Camel</u> can <u>survive</u> for a <u>long time </u>without (drinking)
     (rakuda)   (ikiru)   (nagai aida)
     water.

Vocabulary

hoka	other
kotaemasu	to answer
setsumeisho	manual
soba	close, near
yakusoku	appointment
yūbe	last night

37
WHETHER OR NOT

Appropriate plain form of verb +

'Da' base of noun /na adjective +

} '~ka dōka' + negative form of verb

Lesson

1. *Kanojo ga kuru ka dōka wakarimasen.*
   -I don't know whether she will come or not.

2. *Nihon e iku ka dōka mada wakarimasen.*
   -I don't know as yet whether I will go to Japan.

3. *Kare ga sō itta ka dōka shirimasen.*
   -I don't know whether he said so or not.

4. *Yamada san ga sengetsu amerika e itta ka dōka shirimasen.*
   -I don't know whether Mr. Yamada went to America last month or not.

5. *Hayashi san no ie kara eki ga chikakatta ka dōka oboete imasen.*
   -I don't remember whether the station was close to Ms. Hayashi's place or not.

Try these:
Complete the following using 'ka~dōka' form.

1. Kara ga sake o nomu.
2. Suzuki san ga kekkon shite iru.
3. Sono hen ga shizuka da.
4. Kare wa genki da.
5. Pītā san ga nihongo ga hanaseru.
   (Peter)

Vocabulary

Amerika	....	America
sono hen	....	around there

38
SOME USEFUL GRAMMATICAL EXPRESSIONS

Lesson

Appropriate noun + 'ni tsuite'
Plain form of verb + 'koto ni tsuite'

1) Regarding, about :'~ ni tsuite'

1. *Sensei wa nihon no shakai ni tsuite hanashimashita.*
   -Teacher told us about the Japanese society.

2. *Sono ken ni tsuite watashi wa nani mo shirimasen.*
   -I don't know anything regarding that affair.

3. *Kare ga kaisha o yameta koto ni tsuite shitte imasu ka.*
   -Do you know (regarding the fact) that he has left the company?

4. *Kare ga raishū kara nihon e iku koto ni tsuite shitte imasu ka.*
   -Do you know (regarding the fact) that he is going to Japan from next week?

2) For one : noun + '~ni totte'

1. *Kanji wa watashi ni totte muzukashii desu.*
   -Kanji is difficult for me.

   (As for me, I find kanji difficult)

2. *Anata ni totte kanji wa muzukashiku naideshō.*
   -Kanji must not be difficult for you.

3. *Watashi ni totte kore wa taihen takai desu.*
   -This is too expensive for me.

4. *Kore wa minna ni totte hitsuyō desu.*
   -It is important (necessary) for everyone.

3) Depending on : '~ni yotte'

1. *Hito ni yotte kangaekata ga chigaimasu.*
   -Way of thinking varies from person to person.
   (depending on person)

2. *Iro no konomi wa hito ni yotte chigaimasu.*
   -Colour choice varies from person to person.

3. *Dezain ni yotte nedan ga chigaimasu.*
   -Price varies depending on design.

4. *Kono densha wa yōbi ni yotte komikata ga chigaimasu.*
   -This train gets really crowded depending on
   the day of the week.

4) For : '(~no) tame ni'
Noun + '~no tameni'
Appropriate form of verb + 'tameni'

1. *Sadō no benkyō no tame ni nihon e ikimasu.*
   -I'm going to Japan to study Japanese tea ceremony.

2. *Nihonjin wa minna kaisha no tame ni hatarakimasu.*
   -All Japanese work for (the sake of) company.

3. *Kuruma o kau tame ni okane o tamete imasu.*
   -I am saving money for buying a car.

4. *Buchō no tame ni kaigi ga okuremashita.*
   -The meeting got delayed due to the
   general manager.

5. *Buchō ga konakatta tame ni kaigi ga ashita ni narimashita.*
   -The meeting has been shifted to tomorrow
   as the general manager did not come.

6. *Atarashii uchi o katta tame ni ima okane ga zenzen arimasen.*
   -I have no money as I have bought a house.

Note: The use of '(no) tame ni' can be broadly classified into
two namely.
1. For the purpose of (sentences 1 ~ 3 above)
2. Due to, on account of (sentences 4 ~ 6 above)

Grammar:

'masu' base of verb + 'kata'   ·   way of / how to / manner of / method of ~

hashi no tsukai kata   :   method of using chopsticks (how to use chopsticks)

aruki kata   :   manner of walking (gait)

kanji no yomikata   reading of kanji (way of reading)

Try these:

Fill in the blank with the appropriate expression discussed in this Chapter.

1. Kekkon-shiki _____ kaisha o yasumimashita.
2. Ikebana _____ setsumei shite kadasaimasen ka.
3. Kaisha _____ anata wa hitsuyō nan desu.
4. Hanashi kata _____ hito no seikaku ga (nature) daitai wakarimasu.
5. Ryokō ni iku _____ arubaito o shite imasu.

Vocabulary

buchō	general manager
chigaimasu	different
daitai	almost
dezain	design
ikebana	flower arrangement
kanji	Chinese character
kekkon-shiki	marriage party (reception)
konomi	liking, taste
komimasu	to be crowded
nedan	price
okuremasu	be delayed
raishū	next week
ryokō	travel
sadō	Japanese tea ceremony
shakai	society
tamemasu	to save
yōbi	the day of the week

39
CALLED ~ : '~TO IU'
THE FACT THAT

Noun / adjective
Appropriate form of verb $\Big\}$ + 'to iu' + noun

Lesson

1. *'Jōzu' to iu eiga o mimashita ka.*
   -Did you see the movie called 'Jaws'?

2. *'Tanaka san' to iu hito o shitte imasu ka.*
   -Do you know the person called Tanaka?

3. *'Akihabara' to iu tokoro o shitte imasu ka.*
   -Do you know the place called 'Akihabara'?

4. *'Made in Japan' to iu hon wa nakanaka omoshirokatta desu.*
   -The book entitled 'Made in Japan' was quite interesting.

5. *Nihon no 'yōkan' to iu okashi o tabeta koto ga arimasu.*
   -I have tried the Japanese sweet called 'yokan'.

6. *'Thank you' wa nihongo de nan to iimasu ka.*
   -How do you say 'thank you' in Japanese?

7. *Nihon wa jishin ga ōi to iu koto o shitte imasu ka.*
   -Do you know that Japan has frequent (many) earthquakes?

8. *Inu ga kirai to iu koto wa arimasen ga, mendōkusai kara katte imasen.*
   -It is not that I hate dogs, but I don't have one as I find it troublesome (to keep a dog).

9. *Nihonjin ga yoku hataraku to iu koto wa yūmei desu.*
   -It is well known that the Japanese work hard.

102

10. *Kanojo ni aitaku nai to iu kimochi wa yoku wakarimasu.*

         -I can very well understand your feeling
         that you don't want to meet her.

Try these:
Translate the following into Japanese.

1. I didn't know that he was <u>hospitalized</u>.
                    (nyūin suru)

2. Did you hear that Diana <u>is no more</u>?
                (nakunatta)

3. I have read the novel entitled 'Yukiguni'.

4. <u>I am looking for</u> one (a person called) Mr. Tanaka.
   (sagasu)

5. It is not that I don't want to go, but I am busy on that day.

Vocabulary

inu	....	dog
kaimasu	....	to keep
kimochi	....	feeling
mendōkusai	....	troublesome
nakanaka	....	quite

40
SEEMS TO : '~ SŌ DESU' '~YŌ DESU'

Lesson (1) 'i' - base of i-adjective
'da' - base of na-adjective   }   + 'sō desu'
'masu' base of verb

1. *Kono tokei wa takasō desu.*

     -This watch seems to be expensive.

2. *(Kono ryōri wa) oishisō desu ne.*

     -This food seems to be delicious, isnt it?

3. *Ano hito wa hima sō desu ne.*

     -That person seems to be free.

4. *Ame ga furisō desu.*

     -It seems like raining.

5. *Kyō wa samui node kaze o hikisō desu.*

     -Since it is cold today, I think (it seems)
     I am going to catch cold.

Note: Adjective 'ii' ('yoi') (good) in case of this form follows special conjugation.

ii- yosasō (seems to be good)

Similarly 'nai' form (plain negative) and 'tai' form (want form) or adjectives and verbs also follow special conjugation.

nai - nasasō (doesn't seem to be there)

tai - tasō (see the example below)

taku nai (negative form) of 'tai' form *taku nasasō* desu.

e.g.). Sono hon wa kono toshokan ni nasasō desu.

     -That book doesn't seem to be available in this library.

Inu wa mizu o nomitasō desu.

     -It seems your dog wants water.

Miyamoto san wa gakusei dewa nasasō desu.

(ja)

-Mr. Miyamoto doesn't look like a student.

Kare wa pātī ni ikitaku nasasō desu.

-He doesn't seem to be keen on going to the party.

Lesson (2)   **Seems to : '~ yō desu'**
noun + 'no'
i-adjective   } **'yō desu'**
na-adjective + 'na'
appropriate form of verb

Note 1:   'Sō desu' expresses the likelihood of something purely based on conjecture by the speaker whereas 'yō desu' expresses the same when the speaker is more sure of something based on first hand or reliable information.

Compare the following sentences with those in Lesson(1)

Note 2:   'Mitai' is the colloquial version of 'yō desu' and it's use is by and large the same.

1.   *Kono tokei wa takai yō desu. (mitai desu)*

-This watch seems to be expensive.

(Compared to 'sō desu' in this case the speaker has the idea that the watch is expensive).

2.   *Kono resutoran no ryōri wa oishii yō desu.*

(mitai desu)

-The food in this restaurant, I am told (I believe) is tasty.

3.   *Ano hito wa hima na yō desu.*

(mitai)

-That person seems to be free.

4.   *Ame ga furu yō desu.*

(mitai desu)

-It seems like raining.

(In this case conditions suggest that there are more chances of rain).

5. *Kare wa marude kodomo no yō desu.*

                  -He is just like a child. (mitai)

Grammar :
Marude : as if
    This expression is usually used as a pair with 'yō desu'.
    e.g. Marude nihon ni iru yō desu. (mitai)

                  -I feel as if I'm in Japan.

    Marude obon to oshogatsu ga issho ni kita yō desu.
      -It is as if obon festival and the new year have come
                        together.

    (Since Japanese have long holidays on these two
    ocassions, this sentence is used when something good
    happens.)

Try these:
Change the following into 'sō desu' and 'yō desu' forms.

1.   Kono apāto wa ii desu.
2.   Ano kuruma wa hayaku nai desu.
3.   Kono hen wa shizuka desu.
4.   <u>Netsu</u> ga arimasu.
     (fever)
5.   Kodomo wa <u>kēki</u> ga tabetai desu.
     (cake)

Vocabulary
        kaze .... cold
        hikimasu .... to catch (cold)

41
HEAR-SAY: '~ SŌ DESU'

Appropriate plain form of noun, adjective, verb + ~'so desu'
: **I have heard, I am told**

Lesson

1. *Kono tokei wa takai sō desu.*
   -I am told that this watch is expensive.

2. *Kono resutoran no ryōri wa oishii sō desu.*
   -I am told that the food in this restaurant is tasty.

3. *Ano hito wa hima da sō desu.*
   -I am told that that person is free.

4. *Ame ga furu sō desu.*
   -I've heard (in weather forecast) that it will rain.

5. *Kare wa kaze o hiita sō desu.*
   -I've heard that he is down with cold.

6. *Sono hon wa kono toshokan ni nai sō desu.*
   -I'm told that that book is not available in this library.

Try these:
Put the following in 'sō desu' form.

1. Kare wa kyō kimasen.
2. Yamada san no byōki ga naorimashita.
3. Hayashi san wa kyō okurete kimasu.
4. Kore wa kare no hon desu.
5. Kono hen wa shizuka desu.
6. Kanji wa muzukashii desu.

Vocabulary

naorimasu .... to get well
toshokan .... library

42
FOREIGN WORDS

Foreign words play an important role in the Japanese lexicon as thousands of words from the major Western languuges, specially English have been adopted. The important feature of these foreign words is that they get totally Japanised, for phonetic, morphological and syntactical reasons. They, therefore, pose more problems to foreigners, specially the English speakers, as they need to be relearnt all over again as Japanese words. Some of the cryptic features of foreign words are as under;

‾ All foreign words are written invariably in Katakana. Therefore, when pronouncing them, they must be pronounced in the Japanese way to make oneself understood by the Japanese.

‾ Meaning of the foreign words is not necessarily the same as in the original language. Their sememic range is often restricted.

‾ There are a large number of hybrid words which are coined by combining Japanese and foreign words, for example: Basutei (bus stop), Supīdo ihan (over-speeding), etc.

‾ Foreign words are often shortened, for example: aisu (ice cream), depāto (department store), hōmu (platform) etc.

‾ Nouns borrowed from other languages are verbified by suffixing Japanese verbs, for example : appu suru (to increase, raise), apurōchi suru (to approach) etc.

Some tips about transcribing foreign words into Japanese.

- Mostly pronunciation in the original language is maintained. For example: Kā (car), Kī (key), Uisukī (whisky), Chippu (tip) etc.

- Due to phonetic limitations, such as no *c*, *d*, *t*, *v* or *l* sound or no single consonants in Japanese, appropriate vowel is added to the single consonant to fit it into the framework of Japanese phonology. For example barubu (valve), Ganjī (Gandhi), gesuto (guest), rajio (radio) etc.

Useful expressions involving foreign words

attendo suru	-	attend to a person
daun suru	-	to be down with a disease
dokutā sutoppu ga kakaru	-	to be advised by the doctor to refrain from (drinking)
enjin ga kakaranai	-	unable to concentrate (in work)
ensuto suru	-	have an engine failure (of the car)
forō suru	-	to follow (a job)
gasu ketsu da (desu)	-	(i) run out of fuel (ii) feel hungry
hādo sukejūru	-	crowded (busy) schedule
mai pēsu de yaru	-	do something at one's own pace
masutā suru	-	to master (a skill, language)
memo suru (also memoru)	-	to note something down
misu o okasu	-	commit an error
nō komento	-	No comment
no tacchi desu	-	I've nothing to do with this
non-sutoppu	-	Non-stop (train, flight)
nego suru	-	to negotiate
ōbā desu	-	(he) exaggerates, overstates
panikku jōtai desu	-	in a state of panic, get panicky

panku suru	-	(i) have a flat tyre.
		(ii) system getting deflated (due to over-crowding)
PR suru	-	publicize, advertise
pēpā doraibā	-	driver on paper only (a person who has a licence but no car to drive)
pointo o tsukamu	-	seize the crucial point of a problem
puresshā o kakeru	-	apply pressure (on a person)
puresshā o kanjiru	-	to feel the pressure
pusshu suru	-	push a matter

Common Foreign Words

Airon	Iron, Press
Aisu	Ice cream
Akuseru	Accelerator
Anime	Animation
Ankēto	Questionnaire
Apāto	Apartment
Apointo	Appointment
Arubaito	Part time job
Arukōru	Alcohol
Bai Bai	Bye bye
Baiku	Bike
Baketsu	Bucket
Barubu	Valve, bulb
Basu	Bus
Batā	Butter
Bazā	Bazaar
Beddo	Bed
Beteran	Veteran
Bideo	Video
Bijinesu hoteru	Business hotel
Bijinesu man	Businessman
Bīru	Beer
Biru	Building
Bisuketto	Biscuit
Bōnasu	Bonus
Bōru	Ball
Botan	Button
Burēki	Break
Chansu	Chance
Chippu	Tip

Dansu	Dance
Demo	Demonstration
Depāto	Department store
Dezāto	Dessert
Doa	Door
Doraibā	Driver
Doru	Dollar
Eakon	Airconditioner
Enerugī	Energy
Enjin	Engine
Ensuto	Engine stop, Engine failure
Erebētā	Elevator
Erīto	Elite
Famikon	Video game
Fasshon	Fashion
Furonto	Front office, Reception (of a hotel)
Garasu	Sheet glass
Garēji	Garage
Gasorin	Gasoline
Gasu	Gas
Gomu	Rubber
Hādo	Hardware
Haiyā	Taxi (cab) hired by the day
Hamu	Ham
Hanbāgu	Hamburger
Handoru	Steering wheel
Hankachi	Handkerchief
Heddohon	Headphone
Heri	Helicopter
Hinto	Hint
Hocchikisu	Stapler
Hōmu	Platform
Hōmushikku	Homesick
Hosutesu	Hostess
Imēji	Image
Infure	Inflation
Interi	Intellectual
Irasuto	Illustration
Jūsu	Juice
Kamera	Camera
Konbini	Convenience store
Karā	Colour
Karendā	Calendar
Kī	Key
Kōhī	Coffee
Koin	Coin
Kone	Connection, Pull
Konsento	Power point, socket
Kūrā	Cooler, AC
Kurimu	Cream

Kyanseru	Cancel
Mania	Maniac
Masukomi	Mass communication
Masuku	Mask
Mētoru	Meter
Miruku	Milk
Mishin	Sewing machine
Moderu	Model
Monitā	Monitor
Nega	Negative film
Nekutai	Necktie
Noirōze	Nervous breakdown
Nōto	Notebook
Nyūsu	News
Ōdā	Order
Ōtobai	Autobike, motorbike
Pajama	Pyjama, night suit
Pāma	Perm
Pan	Bread
Panikku	Panic
Panku	Puncture
Pantsu	Underpants
Pasokon	Personal computer
Patokā	Patrol car
Patoron	Patron
Penki	Paint
Pikunikku	Picnic
Piza	Pizza
Pokeberu	Pager
Poruno	Pornography
Posuto	Mailbox
Potto	Vaccuum flask
Puro	Professional
Risaikuru	Recycle
Raito	Light
Rajikase	Radio casette recorder
Rajio	Radio
Ranpu	Lamp
Rejā	Leisure
Reji	Cash register
Repōto	Report
Rihabiri	Rehabilitation
Risuto	List
Roke	Location (for shooting)
Rokku	Lock
Rōn	Loan
Sābisu	Service
Sakkā	Soccer
Sararīman	Salaried worker
Sekkusu	Sex

Serotēpu	Cellotape
Sētā	Sweater
Sofuto	Software
Sōsu	Sauce
Suchīmu	Steam
Sukūru basu	School bus
Sumāto	Smart
Sūpā	Supermarket, Superimpose, Subtitles
Supīdo	Speed
Supōtsu	Sports
Surippa	Slipper
Sutaffu	Staff
Sutairu	Style
Sutamina	Stamina
Sutēki	Steak
Sutōbu	Heater
Sutoraiki (Suto)	Strike (work)
Sūtsu	Suit
Tāminaru	Terminal
Taoru	Towel
Tēburu	Table
Tekisuto	Text
Tēma	Theme
Terebi	T.V.
Tero	Terrorism
Toire	Toilet
Tonneru	Tunnel
Toraburu	Trouble
Torakku	Truck
Toranku	Trunk
Toranpu	Playing cards
Toransu	Transformer
Torepan	Training pants, sweat pants
Tsuā	Tour
Uisukī	Whisky
Waishatsu	Dress shirt
Wanpatān	Stereotyped
Yotto	Yacht
Yūmoa	Humour
Zubon	Trousers

43
SOME OTHER APPLICATIONS OF 'YŌ'

Lesson (1)   Noun + 'no yō na' + noun : like

1. *Sakuya UFO no yōna mono o mimashita.*
>>> -Last night I saw something that looked like an UFO.

2. *Kono aida eki de Shimizu san no yōna hito o mimashita.*
>>> -The other day I saw a person who looked like Mr. Shimizu at the station.

3. *Tenpura no yōna tabemono wa Indo ni mo arimasu.*
>>> -Eatable similar to tenpura is also available in India.

4. *Kesa kōen de hebi no yōna mono o mimashita.*
>>> -This morning I saw somethingthat looked like a snake in the park.

5. *Kare wa otōsan no yōna kao o shite imasu.*
>>> -He looks like his father.

Lesson (2) Noun + 'no yōni' : Like
    Appropriate form of verb + 'yōni'

1. *Kare wa byōki no yōni miemasu.*
>>> -He seems to be sick.

2. *Kare wa kodomo no yōni famikon de asobimasu.*
>>> -He is glued to the video game like a child.

3. *Sumisu san wa marude zenbu shitte iru yōni furumaimasu.*
>>> -Mr. Smith poses as if he knows everything.

4. *Kare wa itsumo shinde iru yōni nemasu.*
>>> -He always sleeps so soundly as if he is dead.

Lesson (3) Plain negative form of verb + 'yōni' +
appropriate form of verb
: so as not to

1. *Kaze o hikanai yōni ki o tsukete kudasai.*
    -Please be careful so as not to catch cold.
2. *Onaka o kowasanai yōni namamizu o sakete kudasai.*
    -Please avoid tap water so as not
    to upset your stomach.
3. *Kanji o wasurenai yōni mainichi renshū shite imasu.*
    -I practice kanji everyday so
    as not to forget them.
4. *Kaisha ni okurenai yōni hayaku uchi o demasu.*
    -I leave my house early so as not
    to be late for work.

Note: Although this form is mostly used with the first verb in negative but it can also be used with the affirmative form.

e.g. Kaigi ni ma ni au yō ni, hayaku deta hō ga ii desu.
    -You had better leave early so as to reach for the meeting on time.

Hon ga yomeru yōni, atarashii megane o tsukuri mashita.
    -I got new spectacles so as to be able to read.

Lesson (4)   Appropriate form of verb + 'yōni shite imasu'
:to make it a point, try to

1. *Yasai to kudamono o dekirudake taberu yōni shite imasu.*
    -I try to eat lots of
    vegetables and fruits.
2. *Sake o amari nomanai yōni shite imasu.*
    -I have made it a point
    not to drink much.
3. *Maiasa undō suru yōni shite imasu.*
    -I have made it a point to exercise
    every morning.

Lesson (5) Appropriate form of verb + 'yōni naru'
: reach a point

Note: Used when some change takes place gradually.

1. *Mainichi renshū sureba, kanji ga yomeru yōni narimasu.*
> -If you practice kanji everyday, you will be able to read them.

2. *Yatto nihongo ga hanaseru yōni narimashita.*
> -Finally I am able to speak Japanese.

3. *Uchi no kodomo wa yatto hitori de kaimono ga dekiru yōni narimashita.*
> -At last my child is able to go for shopping all by himself / herself.

Try these:
Translate the following into English.

1. Watashi wa maiasa asagohan o <u>shikkari</u> taberu yōni shite imasu.   (properly)

2. Jiko ni awanai yōni ki o tsukete unten shite imasu.

3. Watashi wa <u>Pītā</u> san no yōni nihongo o jōzu ni hanashitai desu.   (Peter)

4. Watashi mo kono yōna kuruma ga hoshii desu.

5. Yatto unten ga dekiru yōni narimashita

Vocabulary

famikon	video game
furumai masu	to behave
hebi	snake
kao	face
kōen	park
kono aida	the other day
kowashimasu	to upset, ruin
megane	spectacles

renshū shimasu .... to practice
sakemasu .... to avoid
sakuya .... last night
shitte imasu .... to know
tenpura .... Japanese dish
tsukurimasu .... to make
yasai .... vegetable

44
PASSIVE FORM

'nai' base of type 1 verbs + 'reru'
'nai' base of type 2 verbs + 'rareru'
'suru' → 'sareru'
'kuru' → 'korareru'

Note: Passive form of verbs in Japanese is also used to express 1) capability and 2) respect for others (see lessons 2 & 3 respectively below)

Note: In passive sentences, indirect object always takes particle 'ni'.

Lesson (1) Passive

1. *Kyō jugyō ni okureta node, sensei ni okoraremashita.*
                              (okoru)
                    -I was scolded by my teacher as
                              I was late for the class.

2. *Kinō Hayashi san wa shachō ni yobidasaremashita.*
                              (yobidasu)
                    -Yesterday Mr. Hayashi was summoned by
                              the president of the company.

3. *Indira Ganji wa keibiin ni korosaremashita.*
                              (korosu)
                    -Indira Gandhi was killed by her
                              security guard.

4. *Kono inu wa kainushi ni suteraremashita.*

                              (suteru)
                    -This dog was abandoned by its keeper.

5. *Dorobō wa keisatsu ni taiho saremashita.*
                    -The thief was arrested by police.

Note: Passive form of verbs in Japanese has a typical usage which is called 'meiwaku ukemi' (Inconvenience caused to the subject of the sentence by the action of indirect object)

e.g.)   (Watashi wa) hisho ni kyū ni yamerarete komatte imasu.
-I am in a fix as my secretary left the job all of a sudden.
(Watashi wa) chichi ni shinarete, taihen desu.
-I'm finding it difficult due to death of my father.
Ame ni furarete, kaze o hikimashita.
-I caught cold as I got drenched in rain.

Lesson (2) Capability

Note: Colloquially this form is preferred over 'koto ga dekiru' discussed earlier. However in case of type 1 verbs "alternate capability form" is preferred over this form. Moreover 'sareru' (from 'suru') is used for respect (see lesson (3) below) and for capability 'dekiru' is used.

e.g. unten suru → unten dekiru

1. *Sashimi wa taberare masu ka.*

-Can you eat sashimi?

2. *Anata wa asa hayaku okiraremasu ka.*

-Can you get up early in the morning?

3. *Konna koto kangaeraremasu ka.*

-Can you think of such a thing (to happen)?

4. *Ashita no pātī ni koraremasu ka.*

-Can you come to tomorrow's party?

Lesson (3) Respect

Note: Also see Chapter 51 on Respective Language.

1. *Kono hon o kaware masu ka.*
(kau)

-Would you like to buy this book?

2. *Kore kara bīru o ippai nomaremasen ka.*
(nomu)

-Would you like to have a glass of beer?

3. *Maiasa nanji ni uchi o deraremasu ka.*
   (deru)
   -What time do you leave your house every morning?

4. *Te o arawaremasu ka.*
   (arau)
   -Would you like to wash your hands?

5. *Nihon de unten saremasu ka.*
   -Do you drive in Japan?

Try these:
Fill in the blank with appropriate passive form and also identify which of the three usages of passive form it is.

1. Dorobō ni saifu o _____ mashita.
   (toru)

2. Kodomo ni megane o _____ mashita.
   (kowasu)

3. Tomodachi ni _____ benkyō dekimasen deshita.
   (kuru)

4. Nihon de onsen ni _____ mashita ka.
   (hairu)

5. Nihongo no uta ga _____ masu ka.
   (oboeru)

6. Kyō no kōen de nani o _____ masu ka.
   (lecture)   (hanasu)

7. Issho ni _____ masu ka.
   (kuru)

Vocabulary

chichi	father
dorobō	thief
hisho	secretary
ippai	a glass of
issho	together
jugyō	class
kainushi	keeper, owner (of a pet)

120

keibiin	securityguard
keisatsu	police
komarimasu	to be troubled
koroshimasu	to kill
kowashimasu	to destroy
kyū ni	suddenly
okorimasu	to get angry, scold
onsen	hot spring
sutemasu	to abandon, throw away
taihen	difficult, troublesome
taiho shimasu	to arrest
yobidashimasu	to call, summon

45
CAUSATIVE FORM

Make someone do something
(Used by elder / senior for junior)

'nai' base of type 1 verbs + 'seru'
'nai' base of type 2 verbs + 'saseru'
'suru' → 'saseru'
'kuru' → 'kosaseru'
Exceptions :   neru → nekaseru
               noru → noseru
               kiru → kiseru (to wear)
               kaburu → kabuseru (to put on a hat)

Note: Also see Chapter 50 on Transitive / Intransitive Verbs. In
        case of verbs which have transitive and intransitive
        forms, transitive form is used instead of causative.

e.g.) oriru (to get down) / orosu (to make someone get down)
(watashi wa) okiru (to get up) / okosu (to wake someone up)

Lesson
1.   *Kodomo ni kusuri o nomasemashita.*
                              -I made my child take medicine.

2.   *Kanai ga byōki datta node, (watashi wa) isshūkan kaisha o
     yasumasemashita.*
                        -Since my wife is unwell, I made her take one
                                        week off (from work).

3.   *(Watashi wa) kodomo ni yasai o takusan tabesaseru yōni shite
     imasu.*
              -I always make my children eat a lot of vegetables.

4. *Tanaka sensei wa itsumo jōdan o itte warawasemasu.*
   -Professor Tanaka always says jokes and makes us laugh.

5. *(Watashi wa) nichiyōbi ni shain o kaisha ni kosasemashita.*
   -I made my staff come to office on Sunday.

6. *Kanja o nyūin saseta hō ga ii desu.*
   -You had better admit the patient in the hospital.

Note: In addition to the above, causative form has following usages as well.

Te form of causative form of verb + 'kudasai' (please let me ~)

e.g.)   Kyō watashi ni okane o harawasete kudasai.
        (harau)
        -Please let me pay today.

Netsu ga aru node kyō yasumasete kudasai.
        -Please let me take off today as I have fever.
        (Above sentence can also be said as under.)

Yasumasete kudasaimasen ka.
        -Would you mind letting me take off?

Yasumasete itadake masen ka. (See Chapter 51)

Try these:
Fill in the blank with appropriate causative form of verb.

1. Pītā san ni kūkō e mukae ni _____ .
   (iku)
2. Hisho ni denwa o _____ .
   (kakeru)
3. Hikkoshi no toki otōto ni _____ .
   (tetsudau)
4. Gakusei ni okyaku san no annai o _____ .
   (show around) (suru)
5. Imōto ni shiken o _____ .
   (ukeru)
6. (Watashi ni) shashin o _____ kudasai.
   (toru)

123

Vocabulary

hikkoshi .... moving, shifting
itsumo .... always
kanja .... patient
nyūin shimasu .... admit in the hospital
okyaku san .... guest, client
otōto .... younger brother
shain .... staff, employee
ukemasu .... to appear (an exam)
waraimasu .... to laugh

46
CAUSATIVE PASSIVE FORM :
IS MADE TO ~

'nai' base of type 1 verbs + 'serareru'
'nai' base of type 2 verbs + 'saserareru'
'suru' → 'saserareru'
'kuru' → 'kosaserareru'

Note: This form is used when the subject of the sentence is made to do something forcibly (against his / her wishes).

Lesson

1. *Kinō no pāti de sake o nomaseraremashita.*
   (nomu)
   -I was made to drink at yesterday's party.

2. *Kodomo no toki, okāsan ni yasai o takusan tabesase raremashita.*
   -I was made to eat a lot of vegetables by my mother when I was a child.

3. *Kono mae no nichiyōbi, kaisha de shigoto o saseraremashita.*
   -Last Sunday, I was made to work in the company.

Try these:
Change the following verbs into the causative passive form.

1. Tēpu o kiku.
2. Pāti de uta o utau.
3. Yoru osoku made benkyō suru.
4. Hito no mae de hanashi o suru.
5. Shiranai hito o mukae ni iku.

Vocabulary

tēpu	cassette tape
no mae de	in front of

47
AUXILIARY VERBS

Lesson (1) Te form of verb + 'shimau'

1) Completion of an action

Note: Colloquially 'te shimau' changes to 'chau' or 'chatta' (in case of past tense) or 'jau' (in case of verbs ending in 'nu' 'mu' 'bu').

1. *Mō kono hon o yonde shimaimashita.*
      (yon jatta)
                    -I have already read this book.

2. *Kare wa mō uchi e kaette shimaimashita.*
      (kaecchatta)
                    -He has already left for home.

3. *Sukkari tsukarete shimaimashita.*
      (tsukare chatta)
                    -I'm really tried.

2) Repent something : do something inadvertently

1. *Kēki o zenbu tabete shimaimashita.*
      (tabe chatta)
        -I ate up (could not resist eating) all the pastries.

2. *Bīru o zenbu nonde shimaimashita.*
      (non jatta)
                    -I had (finished) all the beer (by myself).

3. *Kyō kaimono ni itte, okane o zenbu tsukatte shimaimashita.*
      (tsukacchatta)
                    -I used up all the money while shopping.

Try these I:
Translate the following into Japanese.

1. I've already sent that <u>parcel</u>.
    (kozutsumi)

2. I opened my sister's gift <u>by mistake</u>.
    (machigatte)

3. I have <u>lost</u> your book.
    (nakusu)

4. I have already <u>made the payment</u>.
    (okane o harau)

5. I have forgotten his telephone number.

Lesson (2) Te form of verb + 'oku' : do something in advance

1. *Konban okyaku-san ga kuru kara, ryōri o tsukutte okimashita.*
    -I have cooked the food as I have some
    guests coming tonight.

2. *Ashita made ni taipu o utte okimasu.*
    -By tomorrow, I'll type it out.

3. *Kare ni sō itte okimasu.*
    -I'll tell him so.

4. *Ashita shiken na node, yoku benkyō shite oite kudasai.*
    -Since tomorrow is the exam, please
    study well (in advance).

5. *Shokuji no mae ni ofuro ni hairitai kara, oyu o wakashite oite kudasai.*
    -As I want to take bath before meals,
    please keep the hot water ready.

Note: 'Te oku' is also used to mean 'to leave something in its
    present state'.

e.g.) Kono shorui o kono mama ni shite oite kudasai.
    -Please leave this document as it is.

Try these II:
Match the following and translate into English.

1.	Ryokō ni iku kara	i	kopī o shite oite kudasai.
2.	Ashita pātī ga aru node	ii	ima hanashite okimasu.
3.	Wasureru kamo shirenai kara	iii	doa o shimete okimasu.
4.	Raishū kaigi ga aru node	iv	kippu o katte okimasu.
5.	Samui node	v	nomimono o katte okimasu.

Lesson (3)Te form of verb + 'miru': try, do and see

1. *Tonikaku kare ni atte mimasu.*
   -In any case, I will meet him (and see).

2. *Watashi ga tsukutta ryōri desu ga, tabete mimasen ka.*
   -I have made this dish, would you like to try?

3. *Kono omiyage o ima akete mitemo ii desu ka.*
   -May I open and see this gift now?

4. *Nihon e ichido itte mitai desu ne.*
   -I would like to go to (and see) Japan.
   (how it looks like)

5. *Kono fuku ga au ka dōka kite mimasu.*
   -I will try and see whether this dress suits me or not.

6. *Ano eiga ga omoshiroi ka dōka mite mimasu.*
   -I will watch that movie to check whether it is interesting.

Try these III:
Convert the following into *te miru* form and translate into English.

1. Buchō to hanasu.

2. Ato ikkagetsu gurai sumu.

3. Ichido shiken o ukeru.

4. Tegami o kaku.

5. Shinkansen ni noritai.

Lesson (4)   Te form of verb + 'kuru'
Beginning of a process or continuation of an
action up to current point of time.

1. *Ashita hon o motte kimasu.*

-Tomorrow I'll bring the book.

2. *Pāti ni okusan mo tsurete kite kudasai.*

-Please bring your wife also to the party.

3. *Konogoro atsuku (samuku) natte kimashita.*

-These days it has become hot (cold).

4. *Ame ga futte kimashita ne.*   -It has started raining.

5. *Chotto itte kimasu.*   -I will soon be back.

6. *Tabako o katte kimasu.*

-I will just go and buy cigarettes.

Try these IV:
Translate the following into Japanese.

1. Of late I have put on weight.
   (saikin)   (futoru)

2. Please get me that file.
      (toru)   (fairu)

3. Of late I have started understanding computer.
                  (wakaru)

4. You had better see the house once.
            (miru)   (ichido)

5. City has become clean these days.
            (kirei ni naru)

Lesson (5)   Te form of verb + 'iku'
Action or state that keeps changing from the time speaker describes it

1. *Kono hon o uchi ni motte ittemo ii desu ka.*
   -May I take this book home?

2. *Gohan demo tabete ikimasen ka.*
   -How about having dinner (lunch)?

3. *Okurenai yōni isoide ikimashō.*
   -Let's rush so as not to be late.

4. *Nihon dewa shigatsu kara atatakaku natte ikimasu.*
   -In Japan, it becomes warm (day by day) from April.

5. *Michiko san no tanjōbi ni hana demo katte ikimashō ka.*
   -Shall we buy some flowers for Michiko's birthday?

Try these V:
Translate the following into Japanese.

1. Shall we have coffee <u>somewhere</u>?
   (dokoka)

2. Yesterday I <u>took</u> my children for a movie.
   (tsurete iku)

3. Let's go and see new book in <u>the book shop</u>.
   (honya)

4. You had better eat breakfast (and go).

5. Japenese <u>economy</u> became <u>strong</u> after <u>the 60s.</u>
   (keizai)   (tsuyoi)   (rokujūnendai)

Note: Two other commonly used auxiliary verbs namely, 'aru' and 'iru' have been explained in Chapter 50 on transitive / intransitive verbs.

Vocabulary

aimasu	to suit, fit
akemasu	to open
ane	elder sister
atatakai	warm
ato	another
doa	door
fuku	dress
gifuto	gift
hana	flower
ikkagetsu	for a month
isogimasu	to hurry, rush
itte kimasu	to go (and come back)
katte ikimasu	to buy (and go)
katte kimasu	to buy (and come back)
kippu	ticket
kopī o shimasu	to copy
motte ikimasu	to take (something)
motte kimasu	to bring (something)
natte kimasu	to become
nomimono	drinks
okurimasu	to send
okusan	(your) wife
omiyage	gift, souvenir
oyu	hot water
shigatsu	April
shimemasu	to close
shinkansen	bullet train
sukkari	completely, quite
sumimasu	to live
tabete ikimasu	to eat (and go)
taipu	typing
tsukaimasu	to spend, use
tsukaremasu	to be tired
tsurete kimasu	to bring (a person along)
uchimasu	to type
wakashimasu	to boil

48
COMPOUND VERBS

Lesson (1)   'masu' base of verb + 'hajimeru'
                                :begin to, start to
1. *Tatta ima tabehajimeta tokoro desu.*
                                -I have just started eating.
2. *Kodomo no toki kara kitte o atsumehajime mashita.*
                    -I started collecting stamps since my childhood.
3. *Mō ronbun o kaki hajimemashita ka.*
                        -Have you started writing the thesis?

Try these I:
Convert the following into 'hajimeru' form and make sentences
with the compound verb.

1. oshieru
2. nomu
3. tabako o suu
4. narau
5. benkyō suru

Lesson (2): 'masu' base of verb + 'owaru' (oeru) : finish doing
Note: In this case no distinction between transitive and in-
      transitive verb is made and both mean the same and are
      interchangeable.
1. *Tatta ima tabeowatta (tabeoeta) tokoro desu.*
                                -I have just finished eating.
2. *Yatto ronbun o kakiowari (kakioe) mashita.*
                    -Finally I have finished writing the thesis.
3. *Mō kono hon o yomiowari (yomioe) mashita.*
                    -I have already finished reading this book.

Try these II:
Convert the following into 'owaru' form and make sentences with the compound verb.

1. nomu
2. benkyō suru
3. kiku
4. hanasu
5. kubaru (to distribute)

Lesson (3) 'masu' base of verb + 'sugiru'
:over do, do in excess

1. *Kinō pāti de tabesugimashita.*
   -Yesterday I overate in the party.

2. *Nomisuginai yōni ki o tsukete kudasai.*
   -Be careful not to drink in excess.

3. *Asobisugite, shiken ni ochite shimaimashita.*
   -I failed in the exam as I freaked out too often.

Try these III:
Convert the following into 'sugiru' form and make sentences with the compound verb.

1. Okane   o   tsukau.
2. Atama   o   tsukau.
3. Tabako   o   suu.
4. Terebi   o   miru.
5. Hataraku.

Vocabulary

atama	head, brain
atsumemasu	to collect
kitte	stamp
ronbun	thesis
tatta ima	just now
ochimasu	to fail

133

49
PART I : GIVE, RECEIVE AS AN INDEPENDENT VERB

Lesson (1)   Give: 'yaru' 'ageru' 'sashiageru'
(when first person is the subject)

1. 'yaru' is used for junior.
2. 'ageru' is used for senior or equal
3. 'sashi ageru' is used for senior

1. *Sensei no hi ni watashi wa sensei ni hana o sashiage- mashita.*
                              -I gave (presented) flowers to my teacher
                                     on teacher's day.

2. *Kore wa anata ni sashiagemasu.*
                                   -Let me present it to you.

3. *Sono hon wa tomodachi ni agemashita.*
                           -That book I gave away to my friend.

4. *Otōto no tanjōbi ni tokei o yarimashita.*
                               -I gave a watch to my younger
                                     brother on his birthday.

5. *Maiasa inu ni esa o yarimasu.*
                        -I give the feed to my dog every morning.

Lesson (2): Give 'kureru' 'kudasaru'
(When second person or third person is the subject)

Note: 'Kureru' is used when giver is a member of one's family
       (in-group), equal or junior, whereas 'kudasaru' (kudasai
       masu) is used for a member of the out-group or a senior.

1. *Chichi wa tanjōbi ni tokei o kuremashita.*
                        -My father gave me a watch on my birthday.

2. *Tomodachi ga kono hon o (watashi ni) kuremashita.*
> -My friend gave me this book.

3. *Imōto wa kekkon no oiwai ni shiruku no nekutai o kuremashita.*
> -My younger sister gave me a silk necktie
> as a wedding gift.

4. *Shachō wa kekkon no oiwai ni Hawai made no kōkūken o kudasaimashita.*
> -My boss (president of the company) gave me an
> air ticket up to Hawaii as a wedding gift.

Lesson (3) Receive : 'morau' 'itadaku'
(When giver (second or third person)is the indirect object)

Note: 'Morau' is used when giver is a member of one's family (in-group), equal or junior whereas 'itadaku' is used for a member of the out-group or a senior.

1. *Watashi wa tanjōbi ni chichi ni tokei o moraimashita.*
> -I received a watch on my birthday from my father.

2. *Watashi wa kono hon o tomodachi ni morai mashita.*
> -I received this book from a friend.

3. *Watashi wa kekkon no oiwai ni imōto ni shiruku no nekutai o moraimashita.*
> -I received a silk necktie as a wedding gift
> from my younger sister.

4. *Watashi wa kekkon no oiwai ni shachō ni Hawaii made no kōkūken o itadakimashita.*
> -I received an air ticket up to Hawaii as a
> wedding gift from my boss.

Grammar:
Japanese have a strong feeling of 'insider' (uchiwa) and 'outsider' (sotowa). Usually one's family members, relatives, colleagues (including seniors) form the uchiwa when talking to an outsider. However, when talking directly to a member of the uchiwa, the hierarchy remains all the same.

Try these I:

Fill in the blank with appropriate form of 'yaru' 'ageru' 'sashiageru' 'kureru' 'kudasaru' 'morau' or 'itadaku'.

Note: It is not necessary that only one particular verb can be used in a blank. Try different verbs and note the change in meaning.

1. Watashi wa Hayashi san ni jisho o _____.

2. Hayashi san wa watashi ni jisho o _____.

3. Watashi wa maiasa hana ni mizu o _____.

4. Sensei wa watashi ni nihongo no hon o _____.

5. Watashi wa sensei ni nihongo no hon o _____.

6. (Anata wa) dare ni kono nihongo no hon o _____ ka.

7. Dare ga anata ni kono nihongo no hon o _____ ka.

Vocabulary

chichi	my father
esa	food (for animals)
Hawai	Hawaii
hi	day
kekkon	marriage
kōkūken	air ticket
nekutai	necktie
oiwai	gift
shiruku	silk

PART II: GIVE, RECEIVE AS AN AUXILIARY VERB

Note: When these verbs are used as auxiliary verbs their original meaning of giving or receiving is not always reflected in the English translation, as their use is quite typical to Japanese.

Lesson (1) Give: te form of verb + appropriate form of 'yaru' 'ageru' (Doing somebody a favour)

Note: 'Sashiageru' is used mostly independently as in Part I.

1. *Watashi wa kodomo ni hon o yonde yarimashita.*
   -I read out the book to my child.

2. *Watashi wa otōto ni kutsu o katte yarimashita.*
   -I bought my younger brother a pair of shoes.

3. *Hikkoshi no toki, watashi wa tomodachi o tetsudatte agemashita.*
   -I helped my friend in shifting (the house).

4. *Kinō watashi wa Suzuki san ni o-kane o kashite agemashita.*
   -I lent Suzuki some money yesterday.

Lesson (2) Give: te form of verb + appropriate form of 'kureru' 'kudasaru' [Asking someone for a favour ('kureru' informal, 'kudasaru' formal) or appreciating someone's gesture.]

Note: In Japanese when requesting someone directly, negative form of the verb is more polite.

1. *Haizara o totte kuremasen ka.*
   -Would you pass me the ashtray?

2. *Chotto watashi no heya ni kite kuremasen ka.*
   -Would you mind coming to my room?

3. *Otōsan wa (watashi no) shukudai o mite kuremashita.*
   -My father checked my homework.

4. *Nagasaki sensei wa (watashi o) Tanaka san ni shōkai shite kudasaimashita.*
   -Prof. Nagasaki introduced me to Mr.Tanaka

5. *Sumimasen ga, ashita rekishi no hon o motte kite kudasaimasen ka.*
   -I'm sorry but could you kindly get me the book on history tomorrow?

Lesson (3) Receive: 'te form of verb + appropriate form of 'morau' 'itadaku' (getting something done by order/on request)

Note: When directly asking / requesting a person, negative form of the alternative capability form, i.e. 'moraemasen ka' / 'itadakemasen ka' is used.

1. *Watashi wa tomodachi ni bīru o katte kite moraimashita.*
   -I had my friend buy beer for me.

2. *Chotto bīru o katte kite moraemasen ka.*
   -Could you buy some beer on my behalf?

3. *Watashi wa buchō ni suisenjō o kaite itadakimashita.*
   -I had a recommendation letter written by the general manager.

4. *"Buchō, sumimasen ga suisenjō o kaite itadakemasen ka."*
   -Sir, I shall be grateful if you could write a recommendation letter for me.

Try these II:

Fill in the blank with appropriate form of 'yaru' 'ageru' 'kureru' 'kudasaru' 'morau' or 'itadaku.'

Note: Try different possibilities and note the change in meaning.

1. Mō kurai kara, eki made issho ni kite _____ ka.

2. Ashita made ni kore o taipu shite _____ ka.

3. Ashita kaesu kara, ichiman-en kashite _____ ka.

4. Tomodachi ni eki made issho ni kite _____.

5. Kinō Hayashi san ni ichiman-en kashite _____.

6. Anata no denwa-bangō o Tanaka san ni oshiete _____.

7. Dare ga anata ni nihongo o oshiete _____ ka.
   -Yamada sensei ga oshiete _____.

Vocabulary

haizara	....	ashtray
ichiman-en	....	ten thousand yen
mimasu	....	to check
rekishi	....	history
shōkai shimasu	....	to introduce
suisenjō	....	recommendation letter
sumimasen	....	I'm sorry
torimasu	....	to pass, to get

50
TRANSITIVE / INTRANSITIVE VERBS

Lesson (1) *Transitive verb* is one which is accompanied by a direct object and from which a passive form can be obtained (always takes particle 'o').

Intransitive verb is one that indicates a complete action without being accompanied by a direct object (always takes particle 'ga' or 'wa') (See separate list for transitive / intransitive verbs. Since there is no rule per se to distinguish transitive and intransitive verbs, they must be learnt by rote in pairs.)

1. *Mado o shimete kudasai.*   -Please close the window.

   - *Mado ga shimatte imasu.*   -Window is closed.

2. *Gohan o atatamete kudasai.*   -Please warm the food.

   - *Gohan ga atatamari mashita.*   -Food has been warmed.

3. *(Watashi o) go-ji ni okoshite kudasai.*
          -Please wake me up at 5 o'clock.

   Kesa go-ji ni okimashita.   -I got up at 5 o'clock.

4. *Kuruma o tomete kudasai.*   -Please stop the car.

   - *Kuruma ga tomatte imasu.*   -Car is parked (there).

5. *Tokyo tawā o mimashita.*   -I saw Tokyo tower.

   - *Koko kara Tokyo tawā ga miemasu.*
          -Tokyo tower is visible from here.

6. *Kinō ongaku o kikimashita.* -Yesterday I listened to music.

   Tonari no uchi kara ongaku ga kikoemasu.
          -Music from the neighbouring house can be heard (is audible).

Lesson (2) Te-form of transitive / intransitive verb + auxiliary verb 'iru' and 'aru'

'aru': Always used after a transitive verb and implies that the action has been done by someone and resultant state of that action remains (Always takes particle 'ga' or 'wa').

e.g.).1. *Mado ga akete arimasu.*
> -The window has been opened. (by someone)

2. *Doa ni kagi ga kakete arimasu.*
> -This door has been locked. (by someone)

3. *Sat"o wa irete arimasu.*
> -Sugar has already been put. (by someone)

'iru': Always used after an intransitive verb and indicates the present state of a thing. Its use is similar to the present continuous form discussed earlier.

e.g.) 1. *Mado ga aite imasu.*
> -Window is open.

2. *Doa ni kagi ga kakatte imasu.*
> -The door is locked.

3. *Satō ga haitte imasu.*
> -It contains sugar.

Try these:
Select the appropriate verb.

1. Denki o (tsukete, tsuite) kudasai.

2. Totsuzen denki ga (kiemashita, keshimashita). (suddenly)

3. Hayaku (kimete, kimatte) kudasai.

4. Kyōjū ni kono tegami o (dete, dashite) kudasai.

5. Kowareyasui kara, kore o (ochinai, otosanai) yōni ki o tsukete kudasai.

6. Tantō ga (kawarimashita, kaemashita). (in-charge)

7. Kono kusuri o nondara, byōki ga (naoshimasu, naorimasu).

141

Vocabulary

atatamemasu	to warm
dashimasu	to post
go-ji	five o'clock
kagi	key
kakemasu	to lock
kawarimasu	to change
kimemasu	to decide
kowaremasu	to be broken
kyōjū	today itself
okoshimasu	to wake up
satō	sugar
tawā	tower
tomemasu	to stop
tonari	neighbour

51
RESPECTIVE LANGUAGE

Japan being a hierarchical society has a very elaborate respective language. As explained earlier, the concept of 'uchiwa' and 'sotowa' is also applicable here. Respective language can he broadly classified into two parts. One, respective form (for other person's action) and, two, humble form (for one's own action in relation with the listener). To be more precise, when talking to a person about his / her action the former is used, and when talking about one's own action vis-a-vis the listener the latter is used.

Standard differential and humble form of verbs

Honorific Expressions

Deferential Expressions		Humble Expressions
irasshaimasu	ikīmasu	
	kīmasu	mairimasu
	imasu	orimasu
meshiagarimasu	tabemasu	
	nomimasu	itadakimasu
	moraimasu	
nasaimasu	shimasu	itashimasu
osshaimasu	iimasu	mōshimasu
goranni narimasu	mimasu	haiken shimasu
gozonji desu	shitte imasu	zonjite orimasu
gozonji arimasen	shirimasen	zonjimasen
	kikimasu	
	hōmon shimasu (to visit)	ukagaimasu
oyasumi ni narimasu	nemasu	
	aimasu	omeni kakarimasu
	misemasu	omeni kakeru
omotome ni narimasu	kaimasu	
omeshi ni narimasu	kimasu	
okake kudasai	suwatte kudasai	
oide kudasai	kite kudasai	

143

Family and Relatives : Kazoku to Shinseki

	Deferential Expression		Deferential Expression
ryōshin	goryōshin	kazoku	gokazoku
chichi	otōsan	shinseki	goshinseki
haha	okāsan		
musuko	musuko san		
musume	musume san		
muko (son-in-law)	omuko san		
yome	oyome san		
(daughter-in-law)			
kyōdai	gokyōdai		
ane	onēsan		
ani	onīsan		
sofu (grandfather)	ojīsan		
sobo (grandmother)	obāsan		
mago	omagosan		
(grandson/grand			
daughter)			
oji (uncle)	ojisan		
oba (aunt)	obasan		
oi (nephew)	oigo san		
mei (niece)	meigo san		
gifu	giri no otōsan		
(father-in-law)			
gibo	giri no okāsan		
(mother-in-law)			

Lesson (1)

1. *Hayashi san wa ashita nanji ni irasshaimasu ka.*

    (from 'kuru')

    -Mr. Hayashi, What time will you come tomorrow?

    - *Jū-ji ni mairimasu.*

    (from 'kuru')

    -I'll come at ten o'clock.

2. *Dōzo meshiagatte kudasai.*
    (from 'taberu')

    -Please have (eat) it.

    - *Hai, itadakimasu.*
      (from 'taberu')

    -Thank you (I'll have it).

3. *Takahashi shachō wa irasshaimasu ka.*
    (from 'iru')

    -Is President Takahashi in?

    - *Hai, orimasu.*
      (from 'iru')

    -Yes, he is in.

    - *(Iie) tadaima dete orimasu.*

    -No, he is out.

4. *Onamae wa nan to osshaimasu ka.*
    (from 'iu')

    -May I know your name?

    -*Watashi wa Ri to mōshimasu.*
    (from 'iu')

    -I'm Lee.

5. *Satō san, kono kiji o goran ni narimashita ka.*
    (from 'miru')

    -Mr. Sato, did you see this article?

    - *Hai, haiken shimashita.*
      (from 'miru')

    -Yes, I have seen.

6. *Pitā san o go-zonji desu ka.*
    (from 'shiru')

    -Do you know Mr. Peter?

    - *Hai, zonjite orimasu.*
      (from 'shitte iru')

    -Yes, I know him.

Lesson (2) In case of verbs other than the above respective / humble form is obtained as under

Respective form: 'o' + 'masu' base of verb + 'ni naru'

e.g.)

kaku	→	o -kaki ni narimasu
hanasu	→	o -hanashi ni narimasu
kiku	→	o -kiki ni narimasu (to listen)
yomu	→	o -yomi ni narimasu

145

Humble form: 'o' + 'masu' base of verb + 'suru'

kaku	→	o -kaki shimasu
hanasu	→	o -hanashi shimasu
kiku	→	o -kiki shimasu
yomu	→	o -yomi shimasu

Note: It may be recalled that passive form of verbs can also be used as respective form.

Lesson (3)

'O': Prefix that expresses politeness. Prefixed to verbs (as seen above), adjectives and nouns to express politeness, respect or humility.

(i)

o-kane	money	o -naka	stomach
o-kashi	sweets	o -rei	gratitude, thanks
o-sara	plate(s)	o -furo	bath
o-yu	hot water	o -share	fashionable
o-cha	tea		
o-hashi	chopsticks		
o-tearai	toilet		

Note: Above forms have become standard and are inconceivable without 'o'.

(ii) In Japanese in principle, pronoun 'anata' (you) is avoided when directly talking to a person, as it is considered to be rude. Another reason could be that it is used by wives to address their husbands, although it is gradually going out of fashion as these days wives call their husbands by first name.

1. *O-namae wa (nan desu ka).*
   -What is your name?

2. *O-shigoto wa (nan desu ka).*
   -What is your occupation?

3. *O-toshi wa (ikutsu desu ka)* -How old are you?

4. *O-sumai wa (dochira desu ka)* -Where do you live?

5. *(Nihongo ga) o -jōzu desu ne.*
   -You are good at Japanese.

6. *Aikawarazu o -isogashisō desu ne.*
   -You seem to be busy as usual.

7. *Nihon ryōri ga o-suki desu ka.*

-Do you like Japanese food?

8. *Noriko san, o-denwa desu yo.*   -Noriko, call for you.

9. *O-tegami arigatō gozaimashita.*   -Thanks for the letter.

Note: In all the above sentences, 'o' is replacing 'anata'. Also see the note on 'go' below.
There is another prefix 'go' which has same usage as 'o' but is basically prefixed to words of chinese origin.

1) go-han -rice, meal
go-chisō-delicious food
go-kigen- health

2) Note: Like 'o', 'go' is also used to replace 'anata'.
Go-kazoku wa nannin desu ka.
   -How many members are there in your family?
(Watashi ga anata o) go-annai itashimashō ka.
   -May I guide you?
Go-teinei ni arigatō gozaimashita.
   -Thank you for your kindness.

Try these:
Fill in the blank with appropriate respective form of the verb.
(Situation: Mr. Yamada and Mr. Lee are meeting for the first time.)

Yamada: Hajimemashite. (Watashi wa) Yamada to ___(1)___.
                                        (iimasu)

Lee: Hajimemashite. Lee to ___(2)___.
                         (iimasu)
Yoroshiku onegai ___(3)___.
                   (shimasu)

Yamada: ___(4)___wa dochira desu ka.
          (kuni)

Lee: Kankoku kara ___(5)___.
               (kimashita)

Yamada: Itsu nihon e ___(6)___ ka.
             (kimashita)

Leé: Kyonen no jūgatsu ni _____(7)_____.
           (kimashita)

Yamada: _____(8)_____ wa nan desu ka.
        (shigoto)

Lee: Mitsubishi de enjinia o _____(9)_____.
           (shite imasu)

Yamada: Sō desu ka. Hanashi wa kawari masu ga, nihon ryōri
       o _____(10)_____ ka.
        (tabemasu)

Lee: Hai, nan demo taberaremasu.

Yamada: Nani ga _____(11)_____ desu ka.
          (suki)

Lee: Sashimi to tōfu ga suki desu.

Yamada: Yasumi no hi wa nani o _____(12)_____ ka.
           (shite imasu)

Lee: Taitei gorufu o shite imasu.

Yamada: Sō desuka. Watashi mo gorufu ga daisuki desu.
       Kondo issho ni gorufu ni _____(13)_____.
               (iku)

Lee: Zehi _____(14)_____ sasete kudasai.
        (issho)

Vocabulary

aikawarazu	as usual
annai shimasu	to guide
daisuki	like very much
dōzo	please
enjinia	engineer
gorufu	golf
hanashi	topic
jūgatsu	October
kankoku	South Korea
kazoku	family
kiji	article
kuni	country
kyonen	last year
sumai	residence

148

tadaima .... just now
taitei .... most of time, usually
teinei .... polite
tōfu .... soya beans cake
toshi .... age
yoroshiku onegai shimasu ..... Nice to meet you

52
CONDITIONAL FORM

Lesson (1) 'To':

$$\left.\begin{array}{l}\text{plain form of verb} \\ \text{adjective} \\ \text{noun}\end{array}\right\} + \text{'to' (if, when)}$$

Note: 'To' is used when the outcome is natural or uncontrollable.

1. *Jūnigatsu ni naru to samuku narimasu.*
   -It becomes cold in December.

2. *Kono botan o osu to oyu ga demasu.*
   -If you press this button, hot water will come out.

3. *Tabako o suwanai to ochitsukimasen.*
   -If I don't smoke, I feel restless.

4. *Gakusei da to niwari biki ni narimasu.*
   -We give 20% discount to students.

5. *Takai to kaemasen.*
   -If it is expensive, I can not buy.

6. *Ichiman-en ijō da to kaemasen.*
   -I can not buy if it is more than 10,000 yen.

7. *Isoganai to dame desu.*
   -You (we) must rush.

8. *Sō da to iin desu ga...*
   -I wish it is so.

Lesson (2) 'Ba':

'masu' base of alternative capability
form of type 1 verbs + 'ba'
'masu' base of type 2 verbs + 'reba'
'i' base of i-adjective + 'kereba'
'kuru' → 'kureba'
'suru' → 'sureba'

Note: In many-a-cases, the usage of 'tara' is similar to 'ba'.
Compare the following sentences with those in lesson 3.

1. *Jikan ga areba asobini kite kudasai.*
                    -Please do come over if you have time.
2. *Isogeba maniau deshō.*
                    -If you rush, perhaps you can make it.
3. *Dekireba ashita kite hoshii desu.*
                    -If possible, I would like you to come tomorrow.
4. *Yoku mireba wakarimasu.*
                    -If you observe it carefully, you will understand.
5. *Yasukereba kaimasu.*
                    -I'll buy if it is cheap.
6. *Ikitaku nakereba, ikanakute mo ii desu.*
                    -You need not go if you don't want to.
7. *Chanto yatte kurereba ii desu ga...*
                    -I hope he does it properly.
                    (I'll be happy if he does it properly)
8. *Motto hayaku ieba ii noni...*
                    -You should have told me earlier.

Note: 'ba' form + 'ii noni' is a pattern used colloquially when
the speaker is unhappy with the action/ in-action of the
listener or a person who is the subject of the talk or
because the speaker feels that he could have helped in
changing the outcome.

e.g.) Kaeba ii noni.
                    -Why don't you buy it, (if you want to)?
Jibun de yareba ii noni.
                    -Why don't you do it yourself?
                    or He could have done it himself.

151

Lesson (3) 'Tara'/'Dara': Conditional
ta/da (plain past) base of verbs/adjectives / nouns + tara (dara)

Part 1

1. *Jikan ga attara asobini kite kudasai.*
   -Please do come over if you have time.

2. *Isoidara maniau deshō.*
   -If you rush, perhaps you can make it.

3. *Dekitara ashita kite kudasai.*
   -If possible, I would like you to come tomorrow.

4. *Yoku mitara wakarimasu.*
   -If you observe it carefully, you will understand.

5. *Yasukattara kaimasu.*
   -I'll buy if it is cheap.

6. *Ikitaku nakattara ikanakutemo ii desu.*
   -You need not go if you don't want to.

7. *Ashita ame dattara ikimasen.*
   -I will not go if it rains tomorrow.

8. *Kare wa nihongo ga jōzu dattara yatotte mo ii desu.*
   -I don't mind employing him, if his Japanese is good.

Part 2 Wishful thinking
Note: In this case, 'moshi' (if) and 'tara' form are used as a
   pair. But 'moshi' may or may not be used, which has no
   bearing on the meaning.

1. *(Moshi) okane ga attara, bentsu o kaitai desu.*
   -If I had money, I would like to buy a Mercedes.

2. *(Moshi) yasumi ga toretara, watashi mo iketa noni.*
   -I wish I could also take leave and go with
   others (on the trip).

3. *(Moshi) ano jiko ga okoranakattara kare wa ikite ita noni...*
   -If that accident had not taken place,
   he had been alive.

Part 3 When (same as 'toki')
1. *Jū-ji ni nattara kaerimasu.*
   -I'll go back at 10 (when it is 10).

152

2. *Tabe owattara watashi no heya ni kite kudasai.*

   -After you have finished eating, please come to my room.

3. *Kinō eiga o mi ni ittara, battari Kim san ni aimashita.*

   -Yesterday I bumped into Mr. Kim when I went to see a movie.

4. *Nihon e ittara, nihongo o benkyō shiyō to omotte imasu.*

   -I'm thinking of studying Japanese when I go to Japan.

Lesson (4) 'Nara'

plain form of verb
adjective $\Big\}$ + 'nara' (= if)
noun

Note: Its use is by and large similar to 'ba' and 'tara' forms but it is definitely preferred in case of nouns.

1. *Minna ga nomu nara, watashi mo chotto dake nomimasu.*

   -If everybody is drinking, I will also have some.

2. *Yasui nara kattemo ii desu.*

   -I don't mind buying if it is cheap.

3. *Konpyūta nara Akihabara ga ii desu.*

   -If it is computer, Akihabara is the right place. (to buy)

4. *Anata nara dō shimasu ka.*

   -What will you do in such a situation?

5. *Hitsuyō nara kashite agemasu.*

   -I'll lend you this if you need it.

Lesson (5) 'Baai'

Appropriate plain form of verb +
noun + 'no' $\Big\}$ baai
i-adjective (in case of,
na-adjective+'na' in the event of)

1. *Ame ga futta baai wa pikunikku ni ikimasen.*

   -I will not go on picnic if it rains.

2. *Kaji no baai wa erebētā o tsukawanaide kudasai.*

   -Please do not use the elevator in case of fire.

3. *Ninzū ga ōi baai, futatsu no gurūpu ni wakemashō.*
   -Let us split into two groups if the number is large.

4. *Motto okane ga hitsuyō na baai wa itte kudasai.*
   -Please let me know if you need more money.

Try these:
Fill in the blank with appropriate conditional form.
(it is not necessary that only one form is applicable)

1. Nihonjin wa sake o _____ kao ga akaku narimasu.
   (nomu)

2. Kare ni _____ yoroshiku tsutaete kudasai.
   (au)

3. Tanaka san _____ (watashi wa) yoku shitte imasu.

4. _____ kono kusuri o nonde kudasai.
   (itai)

5. Yoku _____ kore wa okashii desu.
   (kangaeru)

6. Moshi (watashi ga) otoko _____ yakyū no senshu ni
   natta deshō.   (da)   (baseball) (player)

7. Kanojo ga _____ watashi ni shirasete kudasai.
   (kuru)

8. Kaigi ga _____ shokuji ni ikimashō.
   (owaru)

Vocabulary

~biki	~discount
akai	red
battari	by chance
botan	button
chanto	properly
dame desu	must
dekireba	if possible
erebētā	elevator
gurūpu	group
ijō	more than
ikimasu	to live

53
EXTENSIONS OF INTEROGATIVE WORDS

Lesson
Part 1 Suffixing of 'ka'

1. nani → nani ka (something / some)

    1. *Nani ka nomimasen ka.*
        -Would you like to have something to drink?

    2. *Nani ka watashi ni yōji ga arimasu ka.*
        -Do you have some work with me?

2. doko → doko ka (somewhere / anywhere)

Note: Appropriate particle is used after 'ka'.

    1. *Nichiyōbi ni dokoka e ikimasu ka.*
        -Are you going somewhere on Sunday?

    2. *Fairu wa kono hondana no dokoka ni arimasu.*
        -File is somewhere on this bookrack.

    3. *Dokoka de kōhi demo nomimasen ka.*
        -Shall we have coffee somewhere?

3. dare → dare ka (someone)

    1. *Kaigishitsu ni dare ka (ga) imasu ka.*
        -Is someone there in the conference room?

    2. *Kore o dare ka ni agete kudasai.*
        -Please give it to someone.

4. itsu → itsu ka (someday / sometime)
    Mata itsu ka aimashō.
        -Let's meet again (someday).

Part 2 Suffixing of 'mo' (for negation)

1. nani → nani mo (nothing /anything)

1. *Ima nani mo irimasen.*

   -I don't want anything now.
   (for the time being)

2. *Kesa nani mo tabemasendeshita.*

   -I didn't eat anything this morning.

2. doko → doko mo (no where / anywhere)

Note: Appropriate particle is used in between 'doko' and 'mo'.
However its use is optional in some cases.

1. *Nichiyōbi ni doko (e) mo ikimasen.*

   -I'm not going anywhere on Sunday.

2. *Fairu wa doko ni mo arimasen.*

   -File is not to be found anywhere.

3. dare → dare mo (no one / anyone)

1. *Kaigishitsu ni dare mo imasen.*

   -There is no one in the conference room.

2. *Watashi wa kuruma o dare ni mo kashimasen.*

   -I don't lend my car to anyone.

Part 3 Suffixing of 'demo'

nan	→ nan demo (anything)
doko	→ doko demo (anywhere)
dare	→ dare demo (anyone)
itsu	→ itsu demo (anytime)

e.g. nan / dare / itsu / demo ii desu.
-anything / anywhere / anyone / anytime is fine with me.

Vocabulary

hondana	....	book rack
irimasu	....	to need
yōji	....	work

54
RELATIVE PRONOUN

Note : The phrase which explains the features/characteristics of noun must be put into Japanese first with the final verb/adjective of the phrase in the appropriate plain form followed by the noun and the rest of the sentence.

Lesson

1. *Ano se ga takai hito wa dare desu ka.*
   -Who is that tall person?

2. *Ano megane o kakete iru hito wa Robāto san desu ka.*
   -Is that person wearing glasses Mr. Robert?

3. *Kinō pātī de atta hito wa Rī san deshita ne.*
   -The person we met at yesterday's party was Mr. Lee, is'nt it?

4. *Asoko ni oite aru kamera wa ikura desu ka.*
   -How much is that camera kept over there?

5. *Watashi ga katta hon wa kore dewa arimasen.*
   -This is not the book which I purchased.

Try these:
Translate the following into Japanese.

1. Who is the person standing over there?

2. Is there any person who can speak Japanese in your company?

3. Do you know the person who lives in that white house?

4. Could you please get me the bag kept on the chair?

5. The person who is sitting there is the president (of the company).

Vocabulary

kono mae .... the other day
okimasu .... to put
se .... height

tsumaranai .... uninteresting

APPENDICES

160

Part I
COUNTERS (CLASSIFIERS)

COUNTING

There are two ways of counting in Japanese namely.

(i) hitotsu (one), futatsu (two), mittsu (three), yottsu (four),
itsutsu (five), muttsu (six), natatsu (seven), yattsu (eight)
kokonotsu (nine) and tō (ten) and

(ii) ichi (one), ni (two), san (three), yon or shi (four), go (five),
roku (six), nana or shichi (seven), hachi (eight), kyū (nine)
and jū (ten).

Upto ten either of the two can be used, but the former is
essentially used for counting objects that do not have a definite
counter (classifier) and the latter for objects that have a fixed
counter (see the list of counters on the next page).

Beyond ten it is (ii) which is used such as under, jūichi (eleven,
10+1), jūni (twelve, 10+2), jūsan (thirteen, 10+3), and so on.
Twenty is (nijū or two tens), twenty one is nijūichi _ _ _ _ , thirty
is (sanjū or three tens) _ _ _ _ _ hundred is <u>hyaku</u>, thousand is
<u>sen</u> and ten thousand is <u>man</u>.

However, the most difficult aspect of counting in Japanese is the
presence of a large number of counters or classifiers which
differ depending on the object being counted, what complicates
the things further is the euphonic change that classifiers starting
with k, s, h undergo when suffixed after a number. This change
occurs in case of numbers 1, 3, 6, 8 and 10 and subsequently in
case of 11, 13, 16, 18 and 20 and so on.

Note the euphonic change in case of some of the most common
classifiers listed below.

1. KAI : TIMES
ikkai, nikai, sankai, yonkai, gokai, rokkai, nanakai, hakkai,
kyūkai, jukkai

2. KAI : STOREYS
   ikkai, nikai, sangai, yonkai, gokai, rokkai, nanakai, hakkai, kyūkai, jukkai

3. GATSU : MONTH (JANUARY, FEBRUARY...)
   ichigatsu, nigatsu, sangatsu, shigatsu, gogatsu, rokugatsu, shichigatsu, hachigatsu, kugatsu, jūgatsu, jūichigatsu, jūnigatsu

4. KAGETSU : DURATION OF A MONTH
   ikkagetsu, nikagetsu, sankagetsu, yonkagetsu, gokagetsu, rokkagetsu, nanakagetsu, hachikagetsu, kyūkagetsu, jukkagetsu

5. KA (NICHI) : DATES OF THE MONTH
   tsuitachi, futsuka, mikka, yokka, itsuka, muika, nanoka, yōka, kokonoka, tōka, jūichinichi, jūninichi, jūsannichi, jūyokka (14th), jūgonichi... hatsuka (20th), nijūyokka (24th)...

6. NICHI (KA) : DURATION OF A DAY
   ichinichi, futsuka, mikka, yokka, itsuka, muika, nanoka, yōka, kokonoka, tōka, jūichinichi,...

7. YŌBI : DAYS OF A WEEK
   nichiyōbi (Sunday), getsuyōbi (Monday), kayōbi (Tuesday), suiyōbi (Wednesday), mokuyōbi (Thursday), kinyōbi (Friday), doyōbi (Saturday)

8. JI : O'CLOCK
   ichiji, niji, sanji, yoji, goji, rokuji, shichiji, hachiji, kuji, jūji, jūichiji, jūniji

9. JIKAN : DURATION OF AN HOUR
   ichijikan, nijikan, sanjikan, yojikan, gojikan, rokujikan, shichijikan, hachijikan, kujikan, jūjikan...

10. SHŪKAN : DURATION OF A WEEK
    isshūkan, nishūkan, sanshūkan, yonshūkan, goshūkan, rokushūkan, nanashūkan, hasshūkan, kyūshūkan, jusshūkan

11. NEN : YEAR
    ichinen, ninen, sannen, yonen, gonen, rokunen, shichinen, hachinen, kyūnen, jūnen...

12. NENKAN : DURATION OF A YEAR
   ichinenkan, ninenkan, sannenkan, yonenkan, gonenkan,

13. FUN : MINUTES
   ippun, nifun, sanpun, yonfun, gofun, roppun, nanafun, happun, kyūfun, juppun, jūippun, jūnifun...

14. SAI : AGE
   issai, nisai, sansai, yonsai, gosai, rokusai, nanasai, hassai, kyūsai, jussai, hatachi (20), nijūissai (21), nijūnisai (22)...

15. NIN : PERSONS
   hitori, futari, sannin, yonin, gonin, rokunin, shichinin, hachinin, kyūnin, jūnin, jūichinin, jūninin...

16. BAN : ORDER
   ichiban, niban, sanban, yonban, goban, rokuban, nanaban, hachiban, kyūban, jūban, jūichiban, jūniban

17. KO : FOR COUNTING THINGS WHICH DO NOT HAVE A FIXED CLASSIFIER OR ANY SMALL OBJECT (LUGGAGE, EGGS ETC.)
   ikko, niko, sanko, yonko, goko, rokko, nanako, hakko, kyūko, jukko...

18. SATSU : BOOKS
   issatsu, nisatsu, sansatsu, yonsatsu, gosatsu, rokusatsu, nanasatsu, hassatsu, kyūsatsu, jussatsu,...

19. HON : FOR CYLINDRICAL OBJECTS
   ippon, nihon, sanbon, yonhon, gohon, roppon, nanahon, happon, kyūhon, juppon, jūippon, jūnihon...

20. DAI : VEHICLES, INSTRUMENTS, MACHINES
   ichidai, nidai, sandai, yondai, godai, rokudai, nanadai, hachidai, kyūdai, jūdai...

21. MAI : FOR FLAT (THIN) OBJECTS LIKE PAPER, SHEET, BOARD ETC.
   ichimai, nimai, sanmai, yonmai, gomai, rokumai, nanamai, hachimai, kyūmai, jūmai...

22. HAI : GLASSFULL, CUP FULL (SOMETHING FULL OF...)
   ippai, nihai, sanbai, yonhai, gohai, roppai, nanahai, happai, kyūhai, juppai...

163

23. SOKU : PAIR (OF SHOES, SOCKS, STOCKINGS)
issoku, nisoku, sanzoku, yonsoku, gosoku, rokusoku, nanasoku, hassoku, kyūsoku, jussoku...

24. WARI : 10%
ichiwari, niwari, sanwari, yonwari, gowari, rokuwari, nanawari, hachiwari, kyūwari

25. DAI : GENERATION
jū-dai (teen-ager), nijū-dai, sanjū-dai, yonjū-dai, gojū-dai...

26. NEN DAI : AN AGE
gojū nen dai (1950s), rokujū nen dai, nanajū nen dai, hachijū nen dai...

27. BAI : TIMES
ichibai, nibai, sanbai, yonbai, gobai, rokubai, nanabai, hachibai, kyūbai, jūbai...

28. CHAKU : (FOR DRESS OR SUIT)
icchaku, nichaku, sanchaku, yonchaku, gochaku, rokuchaku, nanachaku, hacchaku, kyūchaku, jucchaku...

29. JIN: CITIZEN OF A COUNTRY
Indojin-Indian
Nihanjin-Japanese
Amerikajin-American
Chugokujin-Chinese
Igirisujin-British

LIST OF ADJECTIVES

i-adjective

akarui	(bright)	kurai	(dark)
amai	(sweet)	nigai	(bitter)
atarashii	(new)	furui	(old)
atatakai	(warm)	suzushii	(cool)
atsui	(hot)	samui	(cold)
atsui	(hot, heated)	tsumetai	(chilled)
atsui	(thick)	usui	(thin)
chikai	(near)	tōi	(far)
futoi	(fat)	hosoi	(slim)
hayai	(fast)	osoi	(slow)
hiroi	(spacious)	semai	(small, narrow)
ii	(good)	warui	(bad)
karui	(light)	omoi	(heavy)
nagai	(long)	mijikai	(short)
ōi	(many)	sukunai	(few)
oishii	(tasty)	mazui	(unpalatable, unsavory)
ōkii	(big)	chiisai	(small)
omoshiroi	(mteresting)	tsumaranai	(uninteresting)
takai	(expensive)	yasui	(cheap)
takai	(high)	hikui	(low)
tsuyoi	(strong)	yowai	(weak)
ureshii	(happy)	sabishii, kanashii	(sad)
yasashii	(easy)	muzukashii	(difficult)
yawarakai	(soft)	katai	(hard)

(Some other i-adjectives)

akai	(red)	kowai	(awful)
aoi	(blue)	kuroi	(black)
hoshii	(want)	kuwashii	(detailed)
isogashii	(busy)	okashii	(funny)
itai	(painful)	shiroi	(white)
karai	(spicy)	tanoshii	(pleasant)
kibishii	(strict)	wakai	(young)
kitanai	(dirty)		

na-adjectives

benri	(convenient)	fuben	(inconvenient)
hade	(gay, showy)	jimi	(sober)
jōzu	(good at)	heta	(poor at)
kantan	(simple)	fukuzatsu	(complicated)
kanzen, kanpeki	(perfect)	fukanzen	(imperfect)
shinsetsu	(polite)	fushinsetsu	(impolite)
shizuka	(quiet)	nigiyaka	(lively)
suki	(like)	kirai	(dislike)
yukai	(pleasant)	fuyukai	(unpleasant)

(Some other na-adjective)

fushigi	(strange)	kirei	(beautiful, clean)
genki	(healthy)	mendō	(troublesome)
hima	(free)	seikaku	(accurate, prescise)
hitsuyō	(necessary)	shinsen	(fresh)
iroiro	(various)	taikutsu	(boring)
iya	(hate, dislike)	taisetsu	(important)
jūyō	(important)	tokubetsu	(special)
kiken	(dangerous)	zannen	(regrettable)

BASIC CONJUGATION OF VERBS

Group 1

Dictionary form	'masu' form	'te' form	'nai' form	'ta' form
aru (exist)	arimasu	atte	nai	atta
hanasu (speak)	hanashimasu	hanashite	hanasanai	hanashita
harau (pay)	haraimasu	haratte	harawanai	haratta
hataraku (work)	hatarakimasu	hataraite	hatarakanai	hataraita
iku (go)	ikimasu	itte	ikanai	itta
kaesu (return)	kaeshimasu	kaeshite	kaesanai	kaeshita
kaku (write)	kakimasu	kaite	kakanai	kaita
kasu (lend)	kashimasu	kashite	kasanai	kashita
kau (buy)	kaimasu	katte	kawanai	katta
kesu (switch off)	keshimasu	keshite	kesanai	keshita
kiku (listen)	kikimasu	kiite	kikanai	kiita
kiru (cut)	kirimasu	kitte	kiranai	kitta
matsu (wait)	machimasu	matte	matanai	matta
nomu (drink)	nomimasu	nonde	nomanai	nonda
noru (ride)	norimasu	notte	noranai	notta
omou (think)	omoimasu	omotte	omowanai	omotta
oyogu (swim)	oyogimasu	oyoide	oyoganai	oyoida
shinu (die)	shinimasu	shinde	shinanai	shinda
toru (take)	torimasu	totte	toranai	totta
tsukuru (make)	tsukurimasu	tsukutte	tsukuranai	tsukutta
uru (sell)	urimasu	utte	uranai	utta
yobu (call)	yobimasu	yonde	yobanai	yonda
yomu (read)	yomimasu	yonde	yomanai	yonda

Group 2

Dictionary form	'masu' form	'te' form	'nai' form	'ta' form
deru (go out)	demasu	dete	denai	deta
ireru (put in)	iremasu	irete	irenai	ireta
iru (exist)	imasu	ite	inai	ita
kariru (borrow)	karimasu	karite	karinai	karita
kiru (wear)	kimasu	kite	kinai	kita
miru (see)	mimasu	mite	minai	mitta
neru (go to bed)	nemasu	nete	nenai	neta
oboeru (remember)	oboemasu	oboete	oboenai	oboeta
oshieru (teach)	oshiemasu	oshiete	oshienai	oshieta
taberu (eat)	tabemasu	tabete	tabenai	tabeta
tsukeru (switch on)	tsukemasu	tsukete	tsukenai	tsuketa
wasureru (forget)	wasuremasu	wasurete	wasurenai	wasureta

Group 3

Dictionary form	'masu' form	'te' form	'nai' form	'ta' form
kuru (come)	kimasu	kite	konai	kita
suru (do)	shimasu	shite	shinai	shita

A LIST OF TRANSITIVE & INTRANSITIVE VERBS

Transitive V	Intransitive V	Meaning
Ageru	Agaru	To increase
Akeru	Aku	To open
Arawasu	Arawareru	To appear (Int.V)
		To show (Tr.V)
Atatameru	Atatamaru	To warm
Atehameru	Atehamaru	To apply
Ateru	Ataru	To hit, to guess
Atsumeru	Atsumaru	To gather
Azukeru	Azukaru	To entrust
		To deposit
Chijimeru	Chijimu	To shrink
Chikazukeru	Chikazuku	To bring near (Tr.)
		To draw near (Int.)
Dasu	Deru	To take out (Tr.)
		To come out (Int.)
Fukameru	Fukamaru	To deepen
Fusagu	Fasagaru	To block, choke
Fuyasu	Fueru	To increase
Hajimeru	Hajimaru	To begin, start
Hanasu	Hanareru	To release, leave
Herasu	Heru	To reduce
Hikkurikaesu	Hikkurikaeru	To reverse
Hikumeru	Hikumaru	To lower
Hirogeru	Hirogaru	To spread
Hiromeru	Hiromaru	To spread
Hiyasu	Hieru	To cool, refrigerate
Horobosu	Horobiru	To demolish
Ireru	Hairu	To enter, put in
Iu	Ieru	To say (Tr.V)
Kabuseru	Kaburu	To cover, put on
Kaeru	Kawaru	To change
Kagameru	Kagamu	To bow, bend
Kakeru	Kakaru	has several meanings
Kasaneru	Kasanaru	To overlap
Katamukeru	katamuku	To tilt
Kawakasu	kawaku	To dry
Kegasu	Kegareru	To stain, soil (Tr.)
		To get stained, soiled (Int.)
Kesu	Kieru	To extinguish
Kiru	Kireru	To cut, snap

Kiseru	Kiru	To dress (Tr.)
		To wear (Int.)
Kobosu	Koboreru	To spill
Kudaku	Kudakeru	To crush
Kuttsukeru	Kuttsuku	To stick
Kuwaeru	Kuwawaru	To add (Tr.)
		To include (Int.)
Kuzusu	Kuzureru	To destroy, break, demolish
Mageru	Magaru	To bend
Matomeru	Matomaru	To summarize (Tr.)
		To sum up (Int.)
Mawasu	Mawaru	To spin, turn
Mazeru	Majiwaru	To mix
Midasu	Midareru	To put out of order in disarray (Tr.)
		To be in disarray (Int.)
Miru	Mieru	To see (Tr.)
		To be visible (Int.)
Mitsukeru	Mitsukaru	To find
Mōkeru	Mōkaru	To profit
Morasu	Moreru	To leak
Moriageru	Moriagaru	To heap (pile) up (Tr.)
		To swell (rise) (Int.)
Moyasu	Moeru	To burn
Nagasu	Nagareru	To drain (Tr.)
		To flow (Int.)
Nakusu	Nakunaru	To lose
Naosu	Naoru	To repair (Tr.)
		To get well (Int.)
Naraberu	Narabu	To arrange in order, row.
Narasu	Naru	To ring
Narasu	Nareru	To acclimitize
Nekasu	Neru	To put to sleep (Tr.)
		To sleep (Int.)
Nigasu	Nigeru	To let escape (Tr.)
		To run away (Int.)
Nobasu	Nobiru	To strech, To extend
Nokosu	Nokoru	To remain (Int.)
		To leave (Tr.)
Noseru	Noru	To load (Tr.)
		To board (Int.)
Nukasu	Nuku	To omit
Nurasu	Nureru	To wetten

Odorokasu	Odoroku	To surprise
Okosu	Okoru	To carry out (Tr.V)
		To happen (Int. V)
Orosu	Oriru	To unload (Tr.)
		To get down (Int.)
Oru	Oreru	To break
Osameru	Osamaru	has several meanings
Oshieru	Osowaru	To teach
Otosu	Ochiru	To drop (Tr.)
		To fall (Int.)
Sageru	Sagaru	To lower
Samasu	Sameru	To wake up (Tr.)
Semeru	Semaru	has several meanings
Shimeru	Shimaru	To close
Shizumeru	Shizumu	To drown
Sodateru	Sodatsu	To rear up (Tr.)
		To grow (Int.)
Susumeru	Susumu	To advance,
		To progress, proceed with
Takameru	Takamaru	To increase
Tasukeru	Tasukaru	To help
Tateru	Tatsu	To construct, erect
Todokeru	Todoku	To reach (a thing)
Tobasu	Tobu	To fly
Tokasu	Tokeru	To melt
Tomeru	Tomaru	To stop
Tōsu	Tōru	To pass through (Int.)
		To put through (Tr.)
Tōzakeru	Tōzakaru	To keep away (Int.)
		To go away (Tr.)
Tsubusu	Tsubureru	To break, crush
Tsukeru	Tsuku	To turn on
Tsunageru	Tsunagu	To connect
Tsutomeru	Tsutomaru	To work hard
Tsuzukeru	Tsuzuku	To continue
Ugokasu	Ugoku	To move
Umeru	Umaru	To bury
Uru	Ureru	To sell
Wakasu	Waku	To boil
Waru	Wareru	To break, crack
Wataru	Watasu	To pass, cross
Yogosu	Yogoreru	To stain, dirty
Yugameru	Yugamu	to bend, warp, distort

Verbs that are same in both Transitive & Intransitive Forms:

Genjiru	-	To decrease
Hassuru	-	To discharge, issue, send etc.
Hiraku	-	To open
Masu	-	To increase
Shōjiru	-	To occur

Transitive Verb :   A verb that is accompanied by a direct object and from which a passive form can be obtained.

Intransitive Verb : Verb that indicates a complete action without being accompanied by a direct object.

GREETINGS

Everyday Greetings
1. Good morning - Ohayō gozaimasu
2. Good afternoon - Konnichiwa
3. Good evening - Konbanwa
4. Good night - Oyasuminasai
5. Good bye - Sayōnara
6. See you (tomorrow) - Jā mata (ashita)

Common Greetings
1. Before starting eating - Itadakimasu.
2. After finishing eating - Gochisōsama deshita.
3. When offering food to the the guest - i) Nanimo arimasen ga...
   ii) Dōzo Dōzo.
4. When asked to eat by the by the host - Sumimasen. Dewa enryonaku itadakimasu.
5. When asking the guest to have a second helping - i) Okawari wa ikaga desu ka.
   ii) Okawari dōzo.
6. If you don't want to have more - Mō kekkō desu. Ippai itadakimashita.
7. Asking a guest to be comfortable - Dōzo oraku ni.
8. "Please help yourself" Asking a guest to feel free to eat whatever he likes. - Dōzo goenryo naku.
9. When visiting someone's house, calling out from the entrance. - Gomenkudasai.
10. When entering the house - Ojama shimasu.
11. Welcoming a guest - Irasshaimase.
12. When taking leave of someone - i) Mō sorosoro shitsurei shimasu.
    ii) Dōshitemo ikanakereba naranai tokoro ga arimasu node...

		iii) Hoka ni yakusoku ga aru node...
13.	When thanking someone	- Arigatō gozaimasu.
14.	In response to Arigatō gozaimasu	- Dōitashimashite.
15.	When parting with someone	- i) Shitsurei shimasu. Sayōnara.
		ii) Jā, mata ashita. (so see you tomorrow)
		iii) Gokigenyō.
16.	When going out	- Itte kimasu.
17.	On return from outside	- Tadaima.
18.	In response to "Itte kimasu"	- Itte irasshai.
19.	In response to "Tadaima"	- Okaerinasai.
20.	When someone is going on a trip	- Ki o tsukete itte irasshai.
21.	When you meet a person who has done same favour to you on the previous ocassion.	- i) Kinō wa dōmo arigatō gozaimashita.
		ii) Senjitsu wa dōmo arigatō gozaimashita.
		iii) Konoaida wa dōmo.
22.	When giving a gift	- i) Tsumaranai mono desu ga.
		ii) Kimochi dake desu ga.
23.	When receiving a gift	- i) Itsumo ki o tsukatte itadaite sumimasen.
		ii) Enryonaku itadakimasu.
		iii) Kyōshuku desu.
24.	When wanting to ask about something	- i) Chotto sumimasen.
		ii) Chotto otazune itashimasu ga.
25.	In response to the above "Yes, what is it?"	i) Hai nan deshōka.
		ii) Hai, donna goyō deshō ka.

26.	When requesting someone for something	- i) Sumimasen ga. ii) Osoreirimasu ga. iii) Onegai ga arun desu ga.
	And after having requested him / her	- Yoroshiku onegai shimasu.
27.	Apollogizing	- i) Sumimasen. ii) Gomennasai. iii) Mōshiwake arimasen.
28.	Calling someone out	- Moshi moshi.
29.	Congratulating someone	- Omedetō gozaimasu.
30.	When your colleagues are still working & you return before them	- Osaki ni (shitsurei shimasu).
31.	As you go out of the room, someone else also wants to go out at the same time	- Dōzo osaki ni. (when you offer him to go out first) - Osaki ni. (when you go out first)
32.	When someone thanks you for a small favour	i) Oyaku ni tatete ureshii desu. ii) Tondemo arimasen. iii) Oyasui goyō desu.
33.	Thanking someone	- i) Arigatō gozaimashita (in general). ii) Gokurōsama desu. } Thanks for taking pains iii) Otsukaresama desu. iv) Osewa ni narimashita. (when helped over a long period)
34.	In response to the above	-i) Kochirakoso. ii) Dō itashimashite. (for i & iv only)

35.	When meeting someone after a gap of few days	- Shibaraku desu ne.
36.	When meeting someone after a long gap	- Hisashiburi desu ne.
37.	When you have to pass between 2 persons or in front of a person	- i) Gomennasai. ii) Sumimasen.
38.	When interrupting someone	- i) Ohanashichū desu ga... ii) Sashidegamashii yō desu ga.
39.	When you visit a person and find that he is busy	- Oisogashii tokoro sumimasen.
40.	When you visit a person and he is in the midst of taking his meals.	- Oshokuji chū sumimasen.
41.	When you visit a person on a holiday	- Oyasumi no tokoro sumimasen.
42.	Convey my regards to ~ Remember me to ~	} ~ san ni yoroshiku. Minasan ni yoroshiku.
43.	Nice meeting you	- Oai dekite ureshii desu.

KAZOKU (FAMILY)

Chōjo	-	eldest daughter
Chōnan	-	eldest son
Daikazoku	-	joint family
Giri no okāsan	-	mother-in-law
Giri no otōsan	-	father-in-law
Imōto	-	younger sister
Jijo	-	second daughter
Jinan	-	second son
Kakukazoku	-	nuclear family
Kanai (tsuma)	-	wife
Kyōdai	-	brothers, brothers and sisters
Shimai	-	sisters
Mago	-	grandchild
Musuko	-	son
Musume	-	daughter
Obāsan	-	grandmother
Ojiisan	-	grandfather
Okāsan	-	mother
Onēsan	-	elder sister
Onīsan	-	elder brother
Otōsan	-	father
Otōto	-	younger brother
Ryōshin	-	parents
Shinseki	-	relative
Shujin (otto)	-	husband
Yome	-	daughter-in-law

IDIOMS

Ase o kaku	-	to sweat
Ashi ga omoi	-	to be reluctant to go
Atama ni kuru	-	to get mad (over something)
Bōshi o kaburu	-	to wear a hat
Denwa o kakeru	-	to make a call
Ha o migaku	-	to brush one's teeth
Hana ga takai	-	to be proud
Hi ga kureru	-	to get dark
Kagi o kakeru	-	to lock
Kaze o hiku	-	to catch cold
Me ga sameru	-	to wake up (in the morning)
Me ni suru	-	to notice
Megane o kakeru	-	to wear glasses
Meiwaku o kakeru	-	to trouble (somebody)
Mimi ga hayai	-	to have big ears
Mimi ga itai	-	to make one's ears burn
Nodo ga kawaku	-	to feel thirsty
Ofuro ni hairu	-	to take a bath
Onaka go suku	-	to be hungry
Oyu o wakasu	-	to boil (heat) water
Shashin o toru	-	to take a picture
Shinzō ga tsuyoi	-	to have the nerve to do or say
Shippo o furu	-	to ingratiate oneself with someone
Tabako o suu	-	to smoke a cigarette
Te ni ireru	-	to get something, procure
Te o dasu	-	to get involved with someone or in something
Toshi o toru	-	to become old
Uso o tsuku	-	to tell a lie
Yaku ni tatsu	-	to be useful
Yo ga akeru	-	to dawn

COMMON PROVERBS

1. Hyakubun wa ikken ni shikazu
   - Seeing is believing.
2. Isseki nichō
   - Two birds at one stone's throw.
3. Zen wa isoge
   - Good things must be implemented fast.
4. Gō ni ireba gō ni shitagae
   - When in Rome do as Romans do.
5. Uwasa o sureba kage
   - Remember the devil.
6. Shiranu ga hotoke
   - Ignorance is bliss.
7. Nemimi ni mizu
   - A bolt from the blue.
8. Boketsu o horu
   - Dig one's own grave.
9. Kubi o nagaku shite matsu
   - Wait anxiously for ~.
10. Binbō hima nashi
    - Poor man has no free time.
11. En no shita no chikaramochi
    - Behind the scene performer.
12. Rui wa tomo o yobu
    - Birds of same feather flock together.
13. Ashimoto ni hi ga tsuku
    - Feel the heat.
14. I no naka no kawazu
    - Someone having superficial knowledge.
15. Sumeba miyako
    - Wherever you live you start liking the place.

Part-II
CLASSIFIED GLOSSARY

JAPANESE DISHES

Chāhan	-	Fried rice with egg and shrimps
Chankonabe	-	Stew like dish (mostly eaten by sumo wrestlers)
Chawanmushi	-	Pot steamed hotch potch
Gyōza	-	Fried dumplings stuffed with minced pork
Harumaki	-	Spring rolls
Hiyayakko	-	Tōfu with soy sauce, chopped green onions and grated ginger
Karēraisu	-	Curry with rice
Katsudon	-	Fried pork cutlet on rice
Korokke	-	Croquette
Makizushi	-	Rolled sushi
Miso	-	Soy bean paste
Misoshiru	-	Miso soup
Mochi	-	Cake made with rice
Mugicha	-	Drink made of roasted barley or rye.
Nabemono	-	A large pot simmering over a portable stove from which one eats the ingredients directly, dipping them in citrus and soy sauce
Nattō	-	Steamed and fermented soy beans
Nigirizushi	-	Hand rolled sushi
Nori	-	Dried seaweed (Black paper)
Norimaki	-	Vinegared rice rolled in seaweed
O-sechiryōri	-	Dishes for the new year
Ochazuke	-	Boiled rice steeped in green tea
Ōmuraisu	-	Omlette and rice
Onigiri	-	Rice balls

Pirafu	-	Pilaf, Pilav
Rāmen	-	A big bowl of noodles in soup with lots of seafood, meat and vegetables
Sashimi	-	Sliced raw fish served with soy sauce and grated horse radish.
Subuta	-	Sweet and sour pork
Sukiyaki	-	Beef and vegetables cooked with soy sauce and sugar in a shallow pan
Tempura	-	Deep fried fish, shrimp and vegetables coated in flour batter
Tendon	-	Bowl of rice topped with tempura
Teriyaki	-	Meat, fish cooked in sweet sake and soy sauce
Tōfu	-	Bean curd
Udon	-	Japanese noodle made of flour
Unajū	-	Grilled eel served over rice in a lacquered box
Yakisoba	-	Chow mein
Yakitori	-	Chicken on a skewer
Yakizakana	-	Grilled fish
Yasai itame	-	Stir fried vegetables

JAPANESE CULTURE

Bōnenkai	-	Year end parties
Butsudan	-	Buddhist home altars (used in the home for memorial services for one's ancestors)
Chōchin	-	Paper lanterns used for decoration during festivals and fairs in the shopping centers
Chūgen	-	Mid-year gifts
Chanoyu	-	Tea ceremony
Daruma	-	A doll of a Buddhist priest, Bodhidrama sitting cross-legged in medidation and is a symbol of good luck
Furoshiki	-	Wrapping cloth (usually used to wrap gifts)
Futon	-	Sleeping mats
Geta	-	Wooden clogs (worn with Yukata)
Hanami	-	Flower viewing
Hanko, Inkan	-	Seal used in place of signature
Jinja	-	Shinto shrines
Kakebuton	-	Comforter
Kendō	-	Japanese fencing (sword is made of bamboo)
Kimigayo	-	Japan's national anthem
Kimono	-	Traditional Japanese dress
Koinobori	-	Carp shaped streamers that are hoisted on May 5 by families with son(s) on the roof top of their houses to ensure their success and good health
Kokeshi	-	Wooden doll with round head on a cylindrical body having brilliant colouring
Kotatsu	-	A low table, with a heater attached to its underside, is covered with a thick quilt that hangs to the floor and is used in winter

Mājan	-	Chinese game very popular in Japan
Manzai	-	Comic dialogue between a pair of entertainers
O-mikuji	-	Written oracles with one's fortune printed on them sold at shrines and temples
O-shōgatsu (gantan)	-	New Year
O-shibori	-	Moist hand towel
Obon	-	Traditional annual event, usually celebrated from August 13-15, held for the repose of the soul of the ancestors
Onsen	-	Hot spring
Origami	-	Art of folding of paper into various shapes
Pachinko	-	Pinball machine game - most popular recreation for Japanese
Rakugo	-	Comic storytelling (in a monologue)
Sake	-	Japanese rice wine
Senbei	-	Rice crackers
Sensu	-	Folding fans
Shūgaku ryokō	-	School excussion/Annual study trips conducted in the 3rd year of junior high school and second year of high school
Shikibuton	-	Mattress
Shikki	-	Lacquerware
Shinkansen	-	Bullet Train
Soroban	-	Abacus, a device for calculating
Tatami	-	Flooring mats
Tokonoma	-	Alcoves (space to display a hanging scroll and flower arrangement)
Waribashi	-	Disposable chopsticks
Yukata	-	Unlined cotton kimono (provided in hotels as bath robe)

SICKNESS

Byōki ga naoru	-	Get well
Byōki ni kakaru	-	Fall sick
Chūsha	-	Injection
Fukutsū	-	Stomachache
Geri	-	Diarrhoea
Isha	-	Doctor
Jibyō	-	Old Complaint, Chronic disease
Jōzai	-	Tablet
Kangofu	-	Nurse
Kanzen kyūyō	-	Complete (bed) rest
Kapuseru	-	Capsule
Karada ga darui	-	Feel languid (tired)
Kaze (o hiku)	-	(Catch) cold
Kega	-	Injury
Kibun ga warui	-	Feel sick
Kōketsuatsu	-	High blood pressure
Kōsei busshitsu	-	Anti-biotics
Kossetsu	-	Fracture
Kurumaisu	-	Wheel chair
Kusuri (o nomu)	-	(Take) medicine
Kyūkyūsha	-	Ambulance
Nenza	-	Sprain
Netsu	-	Fever
Nyūin suru	-	(Be) hospitalised
Ope, shujutsu (o suru)	-	(To) operate
Ōto	-	Vomiting
Saihatsu (suru)	-	Relapse (of a disease)
Seki	-	Cough
Shokuyoku furyō	-	Loss of appetite
Taiin suru	-	(Be) discharged
Teiketsuatsu	-	Low blood pressure
Yakkyoku	-	Chemist
Zutsū	-	Headache

PARTS OF BODY

Ago	-	Chin
Atama	-	Head
Chichi	-	Breast
Ha	-	Tooth, teeth
Hana	-	Nose
Heso	-	Navel
Hige	-	Beard
Hiji	-	Elbow
Hitai	-	Forehead
Hō	-	Cheeks
Kaminoke	-	Hair (on head)
Kao	-	Face
Kata	-	Shoulder(s)
Ke	-	Hair (in general)
Koshi	-	Waist
Kubi	-	Neck
Kuchi	-	Mouth
Kuchibiru	-	Lips
Kuchihige	-	Moustache
Me	-	Eyes
Mimi	-	Ear(s)
Mune	-	Chest
O-shiri	-	Buttocks, hips
Onaka	-	Stomach
Oya-yubi	-	Thumb
Senaka	-	Back
Shita	-	Tongue
Te	-	Hand(s)
Tekubi	-	Wrist
Tsume	-	Nail(s)
Ude	-	Arm
Yubi	-	Finger

INTERNATIONAL TRAVEL

Azukeru nimotsu	-	Check-in-baggage
Bakansu (ni iku)	-	(Go for) vacation
Biza	-	Visa
Chokkōbin	-	Direct flight
Dantai ryokō	-	Package tour
Ekusesu	-	Excess baggage
Gaika	-	Foreign exchange
Jisa	-	Difference in time
Jisa boke	-	Jet lag
Kankō basu	-	Tourist Bus
Kankō meisho	-	Tourist spot(s)
Kōkūken	-	Air ticket
Kūkō	-	Airport
Kūkōzei	-	Airport tax
Kyanseru machi	-	Wait listed
Menzeiten	-	Duty Free shop
Omiyage	-	Souvenir
Pasupōto	-	Passport
Purī pēdo takushī	-	Pre-paid taxi
Rikonfāmu (suru)	-	Reconfirm
Ryogae	-	Money exchange
Ryokō gaisha	-	Travel agent
Shinkoku (suru)	-	Declare (at the customs)
Shōtengai	-	Shopping centre
Shucchō	-	Business trip
Sōryōjikan	-	Consulate General
Taishikan	-	Embassy
Tenimotsu	-	Hand Baggage
Yobōchūsha	-	Vaccination
Yoyaku (o ireru)	-	(Make a) booking
Zeikan	-	Customs

HOTEL

Chekku-in (suru)	-	Check-in
Chekku-auto(suru)	-	Check-out
Shinguru	-	Single (room)
Daburu	-	Double (room)
Tsuin	-	Twin (room)
Basu toire tsuki	-	Attached bath and toilet
Chōshoku-tsuki	-	Inclusive of breakfast
Furonto	-	Reception, Front Desk
Gaido	-	Guide
Haiyā	-	Hire a car (by the day)
Hamigaki	-	Toothpaste
Kichōhin	-	Valuables
Kokusai denwa	-	International call
Korekuto kōru	-	Collect call
Messēji, dengon	-	Message
Oyu	-	Hot water
Pūru	-	Pool
Renta kā	-	Rent-a-car
Rūmu-sābisu	-	Room service
Sekken	-	Soap
Shanpū	-	Shampoo
Shigai denwa	-	Trunk call
Shokudō	-	Dining hall
Shoppingu ākēdo	-	Shopping arcade
Taoru	-	Towel
Tsūyaku	-	Interpreter
Yoyaku	-	Booking

POST OFFICE

Bijinesu mēru	-	Business mail, courier
Denpō	-	Telegram (Denpo o utsu -send a telegram)
Fūtō	-	Envelope
Funabin	-	Sea mail
Hagaki	-	Postcard
Insatsubutsu Zaichū	-	Book Post, Printed matter only
Kakitome	-	Registered (Mail)
Kitte	-	Stamp
Kōkūbin	-	Air mail
Kozutsumi	-	Parcel
Nengajō	-	New year card
Shinten	-	Confidential
Shishobako	-	P.O.Box
Shūnyū inshi	-	Revenue stamp
Sōkin	-	Money order
Sokutatsu	-	Speed post
Takkyūbin	-	Door-to-door parcel service
Tegami	-	Letter
Tensō suru	-	Redirect a letter
Yūbin	-	Mail
Yūbin bako	-	Mail Box
Yūbin chokin	-	Postal saving
Yūbin haitatsunin	-	Postman
Yūbin kawase	-	Postal money order
Yūbin kyoku	-	Post office

BANK

Eigyō jikan	-	Working (business) hours
Furikomu	-	Bank-to-bank transfer
Gaika	-	Foreign exchange
Genkin	-	Cash
Ginkō	-	Bank
Ginkōin	-	Bank employee
Honten	-	Head office
Kinri	-	Interest
Kogitte chō	-	Cheque book
Kōza	-	Account (Koza o kaisetsu suru - open an account)
Kyasshu kādo	-	Cash card
Okane o azukeru	-	deposit money
Okane o orosu	-	Withdraw cash
Shiten	-	Branch (of a bank)
Suitōgakari	-	Cashier
Tegata	-	Draft
Teiki yokin	-	Fixed deposit
Tesūryō	-	(Bank) commission
Toraberāzu chekku	-	Traveller's cheque
Tsūchō	-	Pass Book
Zandaka	-	Outstanding balance

TELEPHONE

Daihyō denwa	-	Key number
Denwa chō	-	Directory
Denwa Kyoku	-	Telephone exchange
Denwa bangō	-	Telephone number
Hanashi-chū	-	Engaged
Kakenaosu	-	Redial
Keitai denwa	-	Cellular phone
Kokusai denwa	-	International call
Konsen suru	-	Have a cross connection
(Denwa ga) koshōsuru	-	Telephone going out of order
Kōshū denwa	-	Public telephone booth
Machigai denwa	-	Wrong number
Naisen	-	Extension number
Pokeberu	-	Pager
Rusuden	-	Auto-answering machine
Sen ga kireru	-	Disconnection of line
Shigai denwa	-	Outstation call
Shinai denwa	-	Local Call
Shokugyō-betsu denwachō	-	Yellow Pages
Yobidashi denwa	-	P.P. Number

ESTABLISHMENTS IN A CITY

Byōin	-	Hospital
Danchi	-	Housing complex
Denwakyoku	-	Telephone exchange
Depāto	-	Department store
Dōbutsuen	-	Zoo
Eigakan	-	Movie hall
Eki	-	Station
Gakkō	-	School
Yōchien	-	Kindergarten
Hoikuen	-	Day nursery
Shōgakkō	-	Primary school
Chūgakkō	-	Middle school
Kōkō	-	High school
Ginkō	-	Bank
Kaigan	-	Sea beach
Keisatsusho	-	Police station
Kōban	-	Police box
Kōen	-	Park
Kōkaidō	-	Public hall, Community centre
Kōjō	-	Factory
Kyōgijō	-	Stadium
Minato	-	Port
Shiyakusho	-	Municipal office
Shōbōsho	-	Fire station
Shōtengai	-	Shopping Complex
Sūpā	-	Supermarket
Toshokan	-	Library
Yūbinkyoku	-	Post office
Yūenchi	-	Amusement Park

OCCUPATIONS

Anaunsā	-	Announcer
Bengoshi	-	Lawyer
Bōi	-	Bearer
Bokushi	-	Clergyman
Daiku	-	Carpenter
Denkikō	-	Electrician
Dezainā	-	Dress designer
Dobokugishi	-	Civil engineer
Fujin keisatsu	-	Lady Police Officer
Gādo man	-	Security guard
Gaka	-	Painter
Gyogyō	-	Fishing
Isha	-	Doctor
Kameraman	-	Cameraman
Kangofu	-	Nurse
Keisatsukan	-	Police Officer
Kikaikō	-	Machinist
Kisha	-	Journalist
Kōin	-	Minery
Kokku	-	Cook
Kōmuin	-	Public servant
Moderu	-	Fashion model
Nōgyō	-	Agriculture
Obōsan	-	Buddhist priest
Ongakuka	-	Musician
Pairotto	-	Pilot
Rakunō	-	Dairy farming
Ringyō	-	Forestry
Sakka	-	Writer
Sararīman	-	Salaried worker
Seijika	-	Politician
Senin	-	Sailor
Sensei	-	Teacher
Shinbun haitatsu	-	Newspaper vendor
Shōbōshi	-	Fireman
Shinpu	-	Priest
Suchuwādesu	-	Stewardess
Tarento	-	T.V. personality
Tenin	-	Shop assistant
Uētoresu	-	Waitress
Untenshu	-	Driver
Yūbin haitatsu	-	Postman

SHOPS

Aramonoya	-	Kitchenware shop
Bunbōguya	-	Stationery shop
Denkiya	-	Electrical goods shop
Gakkiten	-	Musical shop
Hakimonoya	-	Clog (footwear) shop
Hanaya	-	Florist
Honya	-	Book shop
Kaguya	-	Furniture shop
Kameraya	-	Camera shop
Kissaten	-	Coffee shop
Kurīninguya	-	Drycleaner
Kusuriya	-	Chemist
Meganeya	-	Optician
Nikuya	-	Meat shop
Panya	-	Bakery
Resutoran	-	Restaurant
Sakaya	-	Liquor shop
Setomonoya	-	Porcelain Shop
Shitateya	-	Tailor
Tokeiya	-	Watch shop
Tokoya	-	Barber
Yaoya	-	Green Grocer
Zakkaya	-	Grocery shop

STATIONERY

Binsen	-	Writing pad
Bōrupen	-	Ball Pen
Bunchin	-	Paper weight
E-no-gu	-	Painting colours
Enpitsu	-	Pencil
Enpitsu kezuri	-	Sharpener
Fairu	-	File
Fūtō	-	Envelope
Gamu tēpu	-	Gummed tape
Hasami	-	Scissors
Hocchikisu	-	Stapler
Inki	-	Ink
Iro enpitsu	-	Colour pencil
Jōgi	-	Scale, Ruler
Kaeshin	-	Lead for Mechanical Pencil
Keshigomu	-	Eraser
Kureyon	-	Crayons
Kurippu	-	Clip
Mākā	-	Marker pen
Mannenhitsu	-	Fountainpen
Memo-yōshi	-	Memo pad
Naifu	-	Knife
Nori	-	Gum, Glue
Serōtēpu	-	Cello tape
Shāpen	-	Mechanical Pencil
Shūseieki	-	Rectifying (white) fluid
Wagomu	-	Rubber band

PERSONAL ITEMS

Beruto	-	Belt
Burausu	-	Blouse
Burezā	-	Blazer
Bōshi	-	Hat
Haburashi	-	Tooth Brush
Hanzubon	-	Knickers
Jaketto	-	Jacket
Janpā	-	Jumper
Keshōhin	-	Cosmetics, Toiletries
Kōsui	-	Perfume
Kushi	-	Comb
Kutsushita	-	Socks
Kutsu	-	Shoes
Megane	-	Specs
Nekutai	-	Necktie
Ōbā	-	Overcoat
Pajama	-	Night suit
Pantsu	-	Shorts
Reinkōto	-	Raincoat
Rōgan kyō	-	Reading glasses
Saifu, Satsuire	-	Purse, wallet
Sebiro	-	Suit
Senmengu	-	Shaving kit
Sētā	-	Sweater
Shatsu	-	Undershirt
Sukāto	-	Skirt
Tokei	-	Watch
Torēnā	-	Track suit
Waishatsu	-	Dress shirt
Yubiwa	-	Ring
Zubon	-	Trousers

HOUSEHOLD EFFECTS

Beddo	-	Bed
Denki Sutando	-	Table lamp
Denshi rēnji	-	Cooking range (Microwave oven)
Denwa	-	Telephone
Doressā	-	Dressing Table
Gasu konro	-	Gas stove
Haizara	-	Ash tray
Hondana	-	Book rack
Jūtan	-	Carpet
Kagami	-	Mirror
Kami dana	-	Household altar (Shrine)
Mishin	-	Sewing machine
Pasokon	-	P.C.
Reibō/Eakon	-	A.C., Airconditioner
Reizōko	-	Refrigerator
Saido bādo	-	Side Board
Sentakuki	-	Washing machine
Sofa	-	Sofa set
Suihanki	-	Rice cooker
Sutōbu	-	Heater
Tēburu	-	Table
Terebi	-	T.V.
Tsūkue	-	Study table
Wāpuro	-	Word processor
Yōfukudānsu	-	Wardrobe

FOOD STUFF/COOKING

Abura de ageru	-	Deep fry
Amai mono	-	Sweet dish
Banshaku (suru)	-	have a drink before meals
Bēkon	-	Becon
Bentō	-	Packed lunch
Butaniku	-	Pork
Demae	-	Home delivery (of food)
Dezāto	-	Dessert
Gyūniku	-	Beef
Hamu	-	Ham
Hikiniku	-	Minced meat
Insutanto shokuhin	-	Instant food
Itameru	-	Stir fry
Kanzume shokuhin	-	Canned food
Karai	-	Spicy thing
Kateiryōri	-	Home made food
Kome	-	Rice
Komugi	-	Wheat
Komugiko	-	Flour
Kōshinryō	-	Spices
Koshō	-	Pepper
Mame	-	Pulses
Maton	-	Mutton
Medama yaki	-	Sunny side up
Musu	-	Steam
Neru	-	Knead
Nikomu	-	Stew
Nyūseihin	-	Milk (Dairy) Products
Okayu	-	Porridge
Omuretsu	-	Omlette
Orosu	-	Grate
Pikurusu, tsukemono	-	Pickles
Reitō shokuhin	-	Frozen food
Sarada	-	Salad
Satō	-	Sugar
Shio	-	Salt

Shoppai	-	Salty
Shushoku	-	Staple food
Sosēji	-	Sausages
Tamago	-	Egg
Teishoku	-	Fixed menu meal
Toriniku	-	Chicken
Yaku	-	Roast
Yōguruto	-	Yoghurt
Yude tamago	-	Boiled egg
Yuderu	-	Boil

FRUITS

Banana	-	Banana
Biwa	-	Loquat
Budō	-	Grapes
Gurēpu Furūtsu	-	Grape Fruit
Ichigo	-	Strawberry
Ichijiku	-	Fig
Kaki	-	Japanese persimmon
Kuri	-	Chestnut
Meron	-	Melon
Mikan	-	Mandarin orange
Momo	-	Peach
Nashi	-	Pears
Orenji	-	Orange
Painappuru	-	Pineapple
Papaiya	-	Papaya
Remon	-	Lemon
Ringo	-	Apple
Sakuranbo	-	Cherry
Suika	-	Watermelon
Sumomo	-	Japanese plum
Zakuro	-	Pomegranate

VEGETABLES

Akakabu	-	Beet
Daikon	-	Radish
Hakusai	-	Celery cabbage
Hōrenso	-	Spinach
Jagaimo	-	Potato
Kabocha	-	Pumpkin
Kabu	-	Turnip
Karifurawā	-	Cauliflower
Kyabetsu	-	Cabbage
Kyūri	-	Cucumber
Nasu	-	Eggplant
Ninjin	-	Carrot
Ninniku	-	Garlic
Pīman	-	Capsicum
Renkon	-	Lotus root
Retasu	-	Lettuce
Shiitake	-	Mushroom
Shōga	-	Ginger
Tamanegi	-	Onion
Tomato	-	Tomato
Tōmorokoshi	-	Corn

FISH

Aji	-	Horse mackerel
Akaei	-	Stingray
Ayu	-	Sweetfish
Dojō	-	Loach
Fugu	-	Swellfish
Funa	-	Crucian carp
Hirame	-	Flatfish
Iwana	-	Char
Iwashi	-	Sardine
Kajika	-	Bullhead
Kajiki	-	Swordfish
Katsuo	-	Bonito
Koi	-	Carp
Maguro	-	Tuna
Manbō	-	Sunfish
Medaka	-	Killifish
Raigyo	-	Snakehead
Saba	-	Mackerel
Sake	-	Salmon
Same	-	Shark
Sanma	-	Saury
Tai	-	Sea bream
Unagi	-	Eel
Wakasagi	-	(Pond) smelt
Yamame	-	Trout

FLOWERS

Ajisai	-	Hydrangea
Asagao	-	Morning glory
Ayame	-	Blue flag, Iris
Bara	-	Rose
Chūrippu	-	Tulip
Hagi	-	Japanese bush clover
Himawari	-	Sunflower
Kānēshon	-	Carnation
Keito	-	Cockscomb
Kiku	-	Chrysanthemum
Kinsenka	-	Marigold
Nanohana	-	Rape blossom
Saboten	-	Cactus
Sakura	-	Cherry blossom
Sumire	-	Violet
Suisen	-	Narcissus
Susuki	-	Eulalia
Tanpopo	-	Dandelion
Tsutsuji	-	Azalea
Ume	-	Apricot, ume flower
Yuri	-	Lily

TREES

Hinoki	-	Cypress
Ichō	-	Maiden hair tree
Kashi	-	Oak
Katatachi	-	Trifoliate orange
Kunugi	-	Kind of oak
Kurumi	-	Walnut tree
Matsu	-	Pine
Momi	-	Fir
Nemunoki	-	Silk tree
Niseakashia	-	Black acacia
Popura	-	Poplar, Aspen
Puratanasu	-	Plane Tree
Satsuki	-	Azalea
Shirakaba	-	White birch
Sugi	-	Cedar
Take	-	Bamboo
Yanagi	-	Willow

INSECTS

Ari	-	Ant
Chōchō	-	Butterfly
Gokiburi	-	Cockroach
Hachi	-	Bee
Hotaru	-	Firefly
Inago	-	Locust
Ka	-	Mosquito
Kabuto mushi	-	Beetle
Kamakiri	-	Mantis
Katatsumuri	-	Snail
Kemushi	-	Caterpillar
Kirigirisu	-	Grasshopper
Kōrogi	-	Cricket
Semi	-	Cicade, locust
Tentōmushi	-	Ladybug
Tonbo	-	Dragonfly

ANIMALS

Buta	-	Pig
Hebi	-	Snake
Hitsuji	-	Sheep
Inu	-	Dog
Kaeru	-	Frog
Kirin	-	Giraffe
Kitsune	-	Fox
Kōmori	-	Bat
Kuma	-	Bear
Neko	-	Cat
Nezumi	-	Rat
Ōkami	-	Wolf
Raion	-	Lion
Rakuda	-	Camel
Risu	-	Squirrel
Sai	-	Rhinoceros
Sakana	-	Fish
Saru	-	Monkey
Shika	-	Deer
Suigyū	-	Buffalo
Tora	-	Tiger
Uma	-	Horse
Usagi	-	Rabbit
Ushi	-	Cow
Wani	-	Crocodile
Yagi	-	Goat
Zō	-	Elephant

BIRDS

Ahiru	-	Duck
Bunchō	-	Java Sparrow
Dachō	-	Ostrich
Fukurō	-	Owl
Gachō	-	Goose
Hakuchō	-	Swan
Hato	-	Pigeon
Hototogisu	-	Little cuckoo
Inko	-	Parakeet
Kamo	-	(Wild) duck
Karasu	-	Crow
Kiji	-	Pheasant
Kitsutsuki	-	Woodpecker
Kujaku	-	Peacock
Mejio	-	Japanese White eye
Niwatori	-	Hen
Oshidori	-	Mandarin Duck
Pengin	-	Penguine
Perikan	-	Pelican
Suzume	-	Sparrow
Taka	-	Hawk
Tsubame	-	Swallow
Tsugumi	-	Thrush
Tsuru	-	Crane
Washi	-	Eagle

COLOURS

Aka	-	Red
Ao	-	Blue
Chairo	-	(Light) brown
Gunjō(Kon)	-	Navy Blue
Hadairo	-	Skin (natural)
Haiiro	-	Grey
Kiiro	-	Yellow
Kimidori	-	Light green
Kogecha	-	Dark brown
Kuro	-	Black
Midori	-	Green
Mizuiro	-	Sky blue
Murasaki	-	Purple
Ōdoiro	-	Ocher (mud) yellow
Orenji, Daidai	-	Orange
Pinku, Momoiro	-	Pink
Shiro	-	White
Yamabuki	-	Bright yellow

Part III
KEY TO SOLUTIONS

Chapter-1

I.

1 Kore wa kamera desu ka.
Kore wa terebi desu ka.
Kore wa isu desu ka.

2. Sore wa anata no kaban desu ka.
Sore wa watashi no kaban desu ka.
Sore wa Suzuki san no kaban desu ka.
Sore wa dare no kaban desu ka.

3. Tokei desu.
Kaban desu.
Jisho desu.
Shinbun desu.

4. Kore wa hon desu ka, jisho desu ka.
Kore wa enpitsu desu ka, pen desu ka.
Kore wa shinbun desu ka, zasshi desu ka.

II.

1. Koko wa Tanaka san no uchi desu ka.

- Iie, Tanaka san no uchi dewa arrmasen.
Suzuki san no uchi desu.

Koko wa uketsuke desu ka.
- Iie, uketsuke dewa arimasen.
Uriba desu.

Koko wa kyōshitsu desu ka.
- Iie, kyōshitsu dewa arimasen.
Jimusho desu.

2. Soko wa māketto desu.
   Soko wa resutoran desu.
   Soko wa tokeiya desu.

3. Kūkō desu.
   Eki desu.
   Watashi no kaisha desu.

4. Doko ga uketsuke desu ka.
   Doko ga yaoya desu ka.
   Doko ga basutei desu ka.

Chapter-2

1. Kore wa taihen amai desu.
   Kore wa taihen oishii desu.
   Kore wa taihen nagai desu.

2. Are wa chotto nigakatta desu.
   Are wa chotto tsumetakatta desu.
   Are wa chotto hosokatta desu.

3. Soko wa amari atarashiku nai desu.
   Soko wa amari chikaku nai desu.
   Soko wa amari atsuku nai desu.

4. Sono ryōri wa zenzen karaku nakatta desu.
   Sono ryōri wa zenzen oishiku nakatta desu.
   Sono ryōri wa zenzen takaku nakatta desu.

5. Ano resutoran wa yasukute, oishii desu.

6. Kono heya wa semakute, kurai desu.

Chapter-3

1. Watashi wa nihon ryōri ga suki desu:
   Watashi wa nihon ryōri ga kirai desu.

2. Kare wa iya na hito desu.
   Kare wa shinsetsu na hito desu.
   Kare wa genki na hito desu.

3. Kore wa hitsuyō dewa arimasen.
   Kore wa taisetsu dewa arimasen.
   Kore wa fukuzatsu dewa arimasen.

4. Are wa zannen deshita.
   Are wa fushigi deshita.
   Are wa kiken deshita.

5. Tokyo wa amari shizuka dewa arimasen deshita.
   Tokyo wa amari fuben dewa arimasen deshita.

6. Kono hito wa shinsetsu de yasashii desu.
   Kono hito wa yukai de omoshiroi desu.

Chapter-4

1. Denwa wa uketsuke no mae ni arimasu.
   Denwa wa uketsuke no soba ni arimasu.

2. Kinō denwa ga arimasen deshita.
   Kinō kaigi ga arimasen deshita.
   Kinō jikan ga arimasen deshita.

3. Kinō no pātī wa hito ga amari imasendeshita.

4. Kyō wa okane ga zenzen arimasen.

Chapter-5

1. Jūni-ji made benkyō shimasu.
   Jūni-ji made yomimasu.
   Jūni-ji made oshiemasu.

2. Kinō unten shimasen deshita.
   Kinō renshū shimasen deshita.
   Kinō yasumimasen deshita.

4. Gohan o tabemasu.
   Miruku o nomimasu.
   Tegami o kakimasu / yomimasu.
   Shinbun o yomimasu / kaimasu.

Okane o karimasu / tsukaimasu.
Kuruma o unten shimasu / kaimasu.
Fuku o kimasu / mimasu / kaimasu.
Nihongo o benkyō shimasu / oshiemasu / naraimasu.

Chapter-6

1. Ame ga futte imasu.
   Onaka ga suite imasu.
   Megane o kakete imasu.
   Okane o haratte imasu.
   Hon o sagashite imasu.
   Kaisha o yasunde imasu.

2. Motto benkyō shite kudasai / shite kudasai masen ka.
   Hon o kaeshite kudasai / kaeshite kudasai masen ka.
   Shigoto o tetsudatte kudasai / tetsudatte kudasai masen ka.
   Denki o tsukete kudasai/tsukete kudasai masen ka.
   Te o aratte kudasai / aratte kudasai masen ka.
   Kaban o motte kudasai / motte kudasai masen ka.

Chapter-7

1. Kirai ni naru.
2. Iya ni naru.
3. Benri ni naru.
4. Taisetsu ni suru.

Chapter-8

1. I want a pen.
2. I don't want a big camera.
3. He wants to go back early.
4. My son wants to become a doctor.
5. I still don't want to eat.

Chapter-9

1. Watashi wa kuruma a unten suru koto ga dekimasu.
2. Watashi wa nihongo a hanasu koto go dekimasen.
   Watashi wa nihongo ga hanasemasen.

3. Watashi wa gorufu ga dekimasu.
4. Watashi wa oyogemasen.
5. Watashi wa kanji ga kakemasen.
6. Tōkute ikemasen.
7. Watashi wa sushi ga kirai de taberu kota ga dekimasen.

Chapter-10

1. Aisu kurīmu o tabenagara eiga o mimasu.
2. Tabako a suinagara denwa o kakemasu.
3. Nenagara shōsetsu o yomimasu.
4. Kōhī o nominagara ongaku o kikimasu.
5. Piano o hikinagara uta o utaimasu.

Chapter-11

1. Kanji wa yominikui desu.
2. Ano hito no hanashi wa wakarinikukatta desu.
3. Kono pen wa amari kakiyasukunai desu.
4. Natsu wa tabemono ga kusariyasui desu.
5. Nihon-ryōri wa tabeyasui desu ga, nattō dake wa tabenikui desu.

Chapter-12

1. Gakkō e iku mae ni gyūnyū o nomimasu.
   Gyūnyū o nonde kara gakkō e ikimasu.

2. Shokuji o suru mae ni shawā o abimasu.
   Shawā o abite kara shokuji o shimasu.

3. Asobu mae ni benkyō shimasu.
   Benkyō shite kara asobimasu.

4. Neru mae ni kusuri o nomimasu.
   Kusuri o nonde kara nemasu.

5. Soto ni deru mae ni denki o keshimasu.
   Denki o keshite kara soto ni demasu.

Chapter-14

1. Tanaka san wa ashita yasumanai to omoimasu.
2. Kono terebi wa yoku ureru to omoimasu.
3. Kare wa mada kite inakatta to omoimasu.
4. Tokyo wa kirei da to omoimasu.
5. Ima Rondon wa samui to omoimasu.
6. Hayashi san wa byōki da to omoimasu.

Chapter-15

1. It is said that Japanese have a long average life span.
2. It is said that this is the best book about Japanese culture.
3. It is said that he didn't come to office yesterday.
4. It is said that drinking (liquor) everyday is injurious to health.

Chapter-16

1. Kachō wa kyō no kaigi ga jūyō da to itte imasu.
2. Hayashi san wa kinō no kaigi ga omoshiroku nakatta to itte imashita.
3. Kanai wa zehi kono eiga ga mitai to itte imasu.
4. Kanojo wa kore wa kanojo no kasa dewa nai to itte imasu.
5. Kare wa gyūniku o zenzen tabenai to itte imasu.

Chapter-17

1. Kyō Suzuki san to iu hito ga kimashita.
2. 'Fuji san' to iu yama ni noborimashita ka.
3. 'Sony' to iu kaisha wa doko desu ka.
4. 'Jaws' to iu eiga wa totemo omoshirokatta desu.
5. 'Sukiyaki' to iu uta o shitte imasu ka.

Chapter-18

1. When I got married, I was 25 years old.
2. When I have my breakfast, I always read the newspaper.
3. When I lived in Japan, I always had my dinner at 7 o'clock.
4. When there are many people, we have a meeting in a big room.
5. When it is troublesome, I eat fast food.
6. When it is raining, I go by my car.
7. When you come to Japan, please give me a call.
8. When you reach Japan, please give me a call.

Chapter-19

1. Kīnō tanjōbi datta node (kara), uchi ni tomodachi ga atsumarimashita.
   - My friends got together at my house as yesterday was my birthday.

2. Ashita pikunikku da kara (na node), hayaku nemashō.
   - Let's go to bed early as there is a picnic tomorrow.

3. Samui node (kara), mōfu o kashite kudasai.
   - Please lend me a blanket as it is cold.

4. Otōsan ga nete iru kara, shizuka ni shinasai.
   - Be quiet as father is sleeping.

5. Kyō wa basu de kimashita. Okane ga nakatta kara (node).
   - I came by bus today. Because I didn't have money.

Chapter-20

1. Wakai noni genki ga arimasen.
2. Kono kaban wa yokunai noni takakatta desu.
3. Ashita wa nichiyōbi na noni kaisha e ikimasu.
4. Kanojo wa onaka ga suite ita noni nani mo tabemasen deshita.
5. Kare wa genki na noni hatarakimasen.

Chapter-21

1. Watashi wa ima no shigoto o yameru tsumori desu.
2. Watashi wa koko ni nagaku sumu tsumori wa arimasen.
3. Teinen taishoku shite kara, chiisai machi ni sumu tsumori desu.
4. Watashi wa isshō kekkon shinai tsumori desu.

Chapter-22

1. Ano machi wa kirei kamo shiremasen.
   - That city might be beautiful.

   Ano machi wa kirei ni chigai arimasen.
   - That city must be beautiful.

Ano machi wa kirei na hazu desu.
- That city ought to be beautiful.

2. Kare wa mada kaisha ni iru kamo shiremasen.
   - He might still be in the office.

   Kare wa mada kaisha ni iru ni chigai arimasen.
   - He must still be in the office.

   Kare wa mada kaisha ni iru hazu desu.
   - He should still be in the office.

3. Kore wa imōto no kaban kamo shiremasen.
   - This might be my younger sister's bag.

   Kore wa imōto no kaban ni chigai arimasen.
   - This must be my younger sister's bag.
   Kore wa imōto no kaban no hazu desu.
   - I'm fairly certain that this is my younger sister's bag.

4. Ano apāto wa hirokute akarui kamo shiremasen.
   - That apartment might be spacious and bright.

   Ano apāto wa hirokute akarui ni chigai arimasen.
   - That apartment must be spacious and bright.

   Ano apāto wa hirokute akarui hazu desu.
   - That apartment ought to be spacious and bright.

5. Ano uchi wa mada aite iru kamo shiremasen.
   -That house might still be vacant.

   Ano uchi wa mada aite iru ni chigai arimasen.
   -That house must be still vacant.

   Ano uchi wa mada aite iru hazu desu.
   -I'm fairly certain that house is still vacant.

Chpater-23
1. I'm just about to go for a movie.
2. I have just had my food.
3. I'm just now writing that report.
4. I was just talking with him on the phone.
5. I was almost killed in a train accident today.

Chapter-24

1. Watashi wa roku-ji made ni okiru koto ni shite imasu.
2. Watashi wa asagohan o shikkari taberu koto ni shite imasu.
3. Watashi wa ryokō shite iru toki, namamizu o nomanai koto ni shite imasu.
4. Watashi wa kodomo no toki, mainichi gyūnyū (miruku) o ippai nomu koto ni shite imashita.
5. Watashi wa byōki no toki, kudamono o takusan taberu koto ni shite imashita.
6. Watashi wa natsu-yasumi ni yama e ikukoto ni shimashita.
7. Watashi wa kuruma (jidōsha) de kaisha e ikanai koto ni shimashita.

Chapter-25

1. Raigetsu kara furui ichimanen-satsu ga tsukaenai koto ni narimashita.
2. Kaisha ni taimu kādo no kikai o ireru koto ni narimashita.
3. Uchi no kaisha dewa minna ga onaji seifuku o kiru koto ni narimashita.
4. Nihon de unten suru toki, keitai denwa ga tsukaenai koto ni narimashita.
5. Watashi no kaisha wa isshūkan ijō yasumenai koto ni narimashita.

Chapter-26

1. Anata wa gorufu o suru koto ga arimasu ka.
2. Anata wa sentaku suru koto ga arimasu ka.
3. Anata wa nihon no shinbun o yomu koto ga arimasu ka.
4. Anata wa sanpo suru koto ga arimasu ka.

Chapter-27

1. Fuji san ni nobotta koto ga arimasu.
2. Kono shōsetsu o yonda koto ga arimasu.
3. Nihonshu o nonda kota ga arimasu.
4. Hikōki ni notta koto ga arimasu.
5. Kuruma o unten shita koto ga arimasu.

Chapter-28

1. Ryōri o tsukuttari, terebi o mitari shimasu.
2. (Kurasu de) bun o tsukuttari, kaiwa o shitari shimasu.
3. Tomodachi no uchi e ittari, tomodachi o uchi ni yondari shimasu.
4. Asagohan o tabetari, tabenakkatari shimasu.
5. Kurasu ni detari, denakattari shimasu.

Chapter-29

1. Tokei o hameta mama ofuro ni hairimasu.
2. Denki o tsuketa mama nete shimaimasu.
3. Tebukuro o shita mama akushu o shite wa ikemasen.
4. Asobi ni itta mama renraku ga arimasen.

Chapter-30

At the hospital

Patient : Sumimasen onaka ga itain desu ga....
Doctor : (After examining)
Sō desu ne. Netsu mo sukoshi arimasu ne.
Kyō wa kaisha o yasunda hō ga ii desu.
Sorekara amari gohan o tabenai hō ga ii desu.
Dekiru dake okayu o tabeta hō ga ii desu.
(Tabete kudasai)
Furūtsu jūsu mo nonda hō ga ii desu.

Patient : Kusuri wa?
Doctor : Futsuka kan dake nonda hō ga ii desu.
(nonde kudasai.)
Sorekara osake wa shibaraku nomanai hō ga ii desu.
Netsu ga aru aida wa ofuro nimo hairanai hō ga ii desu.
Jā, mikka go ni mō ichido kite kudasai.

Patient : Dōmo arigatō gozaimashita.

Chapter-31

1. Shigato ga ōi node doyōbi ni kaisha e konakereba narimansen.

2. Mō jū-ji da kara sorosoro kaeranakereba narimasen.
3. Kono repōto o ashita made ni dasanakereba narimasen.
4. Kaisha ga tōi kara uchi o hayaku denakereba narimasen.
5. Atarashii ie o kau tame ni rōn o karinakereba narimasen.

Chapter-32

1. Zenbu oboenakutemo ii desu.
   - You need not remember all.

2. Kono hon o kaesanakutemo ii desu.
   - You need not return this book.

3. Okane o harawanakutemo ii desu.
   - You need not pay money.

4. Kaisha ni modoranakutemo ii desu.
   - You need not return to the office.

5. Wazawaza koko e konakutemo ii desu.
   - You need not come here all the way.

6. Shinpai shinakutemo ii desu.
   - you need not worry.

Chapter-33

1. Please don't drive car after drinking.
2. Please don't get so angry.
3. At least please don't be absent tomorrow.
4. Please don't use the elevator in case of fire.
5. Please don't switch off the light yet.

Chapter-34

I
1. Tabako o suttemo ii desu ka.
2. Terebi o tsuketemo ii desu ka.
3. Ashita osoku kitemo ii desu ka.
4. Shitsumon shitemo ii desu ka.
5. Kono zasshi o uchi ni motte ittemo ii desu ka.

II.
1. Chiisai jisho demo ii desu.
2. Amari hiete inai bīru demo ii desu.
3. Basho ga fuben demo ii desu.

4. Eki kara tōkutemo ii desu.
5. Apāto ga amari hiroku nakutemo ii desu.
6. Mawari ga kirei dewa nakutemo ii desu.

Chapter-35

1. Ima terebi o mite wa ikemasen.
2. Koko ni chūsha o shite wa ikemasen.
3. Kūkō de shashin o totte wa ikemasen.
4. Unten shinagara keitai denwa o tsukatte wa ikemasen.
5. Hitori de zenbu tabete wa ikemasen.

Chapter-36

1. Anata ni mada kaeranaide hoshii desu.
2. Watashi wa yakusoku shinaide kare ni ai ni ikimashita.
3. Watashi o matanaide hoshii desu.
4. Kare ni issho ni konaide hoshii desu.
5. Rakuda wa mizu nashi de nagai aida ikiru koto ga dekimasu.

Chapter-37

1. Kare ga sake o nomu ka dōka wakarimasen.
2. Suzuki san ga kekkon shite iru ka dōka shrimasen.
3. Sono hen ga shizuka ka dōka wakarimasen.
4. Kare ga genki ka dōka kikimasen deshita.
5. Pītā san ga nihongo ga hanaseru ka dōka shirimasen.

Chapter-38

1. Kekkonshiki no tame ni kaisha a yasumimashita.
2. Ikebana ni tsuite setsumei shite kudasaimasen ka.
3. Kaisha ni totte anata wa hitsuyō nan desu.
   Kaisha no tame ni anata wa hitsuyō nan desu.
4. Hanashi kata ni yotte hito no seikaku ga daitai wakari masu.
5. Ryokō ni iku tame ni arubaito o shite imasu.

Chapter-39

1. Kare ga nyūin shita to iu koto o shirimasen deshita.
2. Daiana san ga nakunatta to iu koto o kikimashita ka.
3. 'Yukiguni' to iu shōsetsu o yonda koto ga arimasu.

4. 'Tanaka san' to iu hito o sagashite imasu.
5. Ikitaku nai to iu koto wa arimasen ga, sono hi wa isogashiin desu.

Chapter-40

1. Kono apāto wa yosa sō desu.
   Kono apāto wa ii yō desu.

2. Ano kuruma wa hayaku nasa sō desu.
   Ano kuruma wa hayaku nai yō dsu.

3. Kono hen wa shizuka sō desu.
   Kono hen wa shizuka na yō desu.

4. Netsu ga ari sō desu.
   Netsu ga aru yō desu.

5. Kodomo wa kēki ga tabeta sō desu.
   Kodomo wa kēki ga tabetai yō desu.

Chapter-41

1. Kare wa kyō konai sō desu.
2. Yamada san no byōki ga naotta sō desu.
3. Hayashi san wa kyō okurete kuru sō desu.
4. Kore wa kare no hon da sō desu.
5. Kono hen wa shizuka da sō desu.
6. Kanji wa muzukashi sō desu.

Chapter-43

1. I try to eat my breakfast properly every morning.
2. I drive the car carefully so as not to have an accident.
3. I want to speak Japanese well like Mr. Peter.
4. I also want a car like this.
5. Finally I am able to drive (car).

Chapter-44

1. Dorobō ni saifu o toraremashita. (Passive)
2. Kodomo ni megane o kowasaremashita. (Passive)
3. Tomodachi ni korarete benkyō dekimasendeshita. (Passive)

4. Nihon de onsen ni hairaremashita ka. (Respect)
5. Nihongo no uta ga oboerare masu ka. (Capacity)
6. Kyō no kōen de nani o hanasaremasu ka. (Respect)
7. Issho ni koraremasu ka. (Capacity/Respect)

Chapter-45

1. Pītā san ni kūkō e mukae ni ikasemasu / ikasemashita.
2. Hisho ni denwa o kakesasemasu/kakesasemashita.
3. Hikkoshi no toki otōto ni tetsudawasemasu/ tetsudawasemashita.
4. Gakusei ni okyaku san no annai o sasemasu / sasemashita.
5. Imōto ni shiken o ukesasemasu / ukesasemashita.
6. (Watashi ni) shashin o torasete kudasai.

Chapter-46

1. Tepū o kikaseraremashita.
2. Pātī de uta o utawaseraremashita.
3. Yoru osoku made benkyō saseraremashita.
4. Hito no mae de hanashi o saseraremashita.
5. Shiranai hito o mukae ni ikaseraremashita.

Chapter-47

I
1. Mō sono kozutsumi o okutte shimaimashita.
2. (Watashi wa) machigatte ane/imōto no gifuto o akete shimaimashita.
3. Anata no hon o nakushite shimaimashita.
4. Mō okane o haratte shimaimashita.
5. Kare no denwabangō o nakushite shimaimashita.

II.
1. Ryokō ni iku kara kippu o katte okimasu. (iv)
   - I'll buy a ticket (in advance) as I am going for a trip.

2. Ashita pātī ga aru node nomimono o katte okimasu. (V)
   - I will buy drinks as there is a party tomorrow.

3. Wasureru kamoshirenai kara ima hanashite okimasu. (ii)
   - I will tell you now as I may forget it.

4. Raishū kaigi ga aru node kopī o shite oite kudasai. (i)
- Since we have the meeting tomorrow, please copy it.
5. Samui node doa o shimete okimasu. (iii)
- I am closing the door as it is cold.

III.
1. Buchō to hanashite mimasu.
- I will try talking to the general manager.
2. Ato ikkagetsu gurai sunde mimasu.
- I will live here another one month (and see).
3. Ichido shiken o ukete mimasu.
- I will apear in the exam (and see).
4. Tegami o kaite mimasu.
- I will try writing a letter.
5. Shinkansen ni notte mitai desu.
- I would like to travel by the bullet train.

IV.
1. Saikin futotte kimashita.
2. Ano fairu o totte kite kudasai.
3. Saikin konpyūta ga wakatte kimashita.
4. Ichido ie o mite kita hō ga ii desu.
5. Konogoro machi ga kirei ni natte kimashita.

V.
1. Dokoka de kōhī demo nonde ikimasen ka.
2. Kinō kodomo o eiga ni tsurete ikimashita.
3. Honya ni atarashii hon o mini ikimashō.
4. Asagohan o tabete itta hō ga ii desu (yo).
5. Nihon no keizai wa rokujūnendai kara tsuyoku natte ikimashita.

Chapter-48
I.
1. oshiehajimemasu
-Watashi wa raigetsu kara nihongo o oshiehajimemasu.
2. nomihajimemasu
-Kodomo wa yatto miruku o nomihajimemashita.

3. tabako o suihajimemasu
   - Kare wa shokuji no ato de tabako o suihajime mashita.
4. naraihajimemasu
   -Watashi wa jussai no toki piano a naraihajimemashita.
5. benkyō shihajimemasu
   -Gakusei wa shizuka ni benkyō shihajimemashita.

II.
1. nomiowarimasu
   -Mō sūpu o nomiowarimashita.
   (soup)

2. benkyō shiowarimasu
   - Yatto kyō no kanji o shiowarimashita.

3. kikiowarimasu
   -Ima anata no kasetto o kikiowatta tokoro desu.
   (cassette tape)

4. hanashiowarimasu
   -Hanashiowaru made matte kudasai.

5. Kubariowarimasu
   - Sensei ga shiken no mondai o kubariowari mashita.

III
1. Okane o tsukaisugimasu.
   -Kinō kaimono ni itte, okane o tsukaisugimashita.

2. Atama o tsukaisugimasu.
   -Nihongo no jugyō de atama o tsukaisugimashita.

3. Tabako o suisugimasu.
   -Tabako o suisugite nodo ga itai desu.
   (throat)

4. Terebi o misugimasu.
   -Terebi o misugite, shukudai ga dekimasendeshita.

5. Hatarakisugimasu.
   -Nihonjin wa hatarakisugimasu.

Chapter-49

I

1. Watashi wa Hayashi san ni jisho o agemashita.
   -I gave a dictionary to Mr. Hayashi.

   Watashi wa Hayashi san ni jisho o sashiagemashita.
   -I presented a dictionary to Mr. Hayashi. (In this case, Mr.
   Hayashi is senior to me.)

   Watashi wa Hayashi san ni jisho o moraimashita.
   - I received a dictionary from Mr. Hayashi.
   Watashi wa Hayashi san ni jisho o itadakimashita.
   -I received a dictionery from Mr. Hayashi. (in this case, Mr.
   Hayashi is senior to me.)

2. Hayashi san wa watashi ni jisho o kuremashita.
   -Mr. Hayashi gave me a dictionery.

   Hayashi san wa watashi ni jisho o kudasaimashita.
   -Mr. Hayashi gave me a dictionery. (In this case, Mr.
   Hayashi is senior to me.)

3. Watashi wa maiasa hana ni mizu o yarimasu.

4. Sensei wa watashi ni nihongo no hon o kudasaimashita.

5. Watashi wa sensei ni nihongo no hon o sashiagemashita.
   -I presented a Japanese book to my teacher.

   Watashi wa sensei ni nihongo no hon o itadakimashita.
   -I received a Japanese book from my teacher.

6. (Anata wa) dare ni kono nihongo no hon o moraimashita ka.

7. Dare ga anata ni kono nihongo no hon o kuremashita ka.

II.

1. Mō kurai kara, eki made issho ni kite kuremasen ka.
   -As it is dark outside, would you come with me to the
   station?

   Mō kurai kara, eki mae issho ni kite kudasaimasen ka.
   -As it is dark outside, would you mind coming with me to
   the station?

Mō kurai kara, eki made issho ni kite moraemasen ka.
(The same meaning, but slightly politer than 'kuremasen ka'.)

Mō kurai kara, eki made issho ni kite itadakemasen ka.
(The same meaning, but the most polite among all.)

2. Ashita made ni kore o taipu shite kuremasen ka.
   -Would you type this for me by tomorrow?

   Ashita made ni kore o taipu shite kudasaimasen ka.
   -Would you mind typing this for me by tomorrow?

   Ashita made ni kore o taipu shite moraemasen ka.
   (The same meaning, but slightly politer than 'kuremasen ka'.)

   Ashita made ni kore o taipu shite itadakemasen ka.
   (The same meaning, but the most polite among all.)

3. Ashita kaesu kara, ichiman-en kashite kuremasen ka.
   -I will return it tomorrow, but would you lend me 10,000 yen?

   Ashita kaesu kara, ichiman - en kashite kudasaimasen ka.
   -I will return it tomorrow, but would you mind lending me 10,000 yen?

   Ashita kaesu kara, ichiman - en kashite moraemasen ka.
   (The same meaning, but slightly politer than 'kuremasen ka'.)

   Ashita kaesu kara, ichiman - en kashite itadakemasen ka.
   (The same meaning, but the most polite among all.)

4. Tomodachi ni eki made issho ni kite moraimashita.

5. Kinō Hayashi san ni ichiman-en kashite agemashita.
   -I lent 10,000 yen to Mr. Hayashi, yesterday.

   Kinō Hayashi san ni ichiman-en kashite moraimashita.
   -I borrowed 10,000 yen from Mr. Hayashi yesterday.

   Kinō Hayashi san ni ichiman-en kashite itadakimashita.
   (The same meaning as 'kashite moraimashita' but this sentence is politer.)

6. Anata no denwa-bangō o Tanaka san ni oshiete agemashita.
   -I have given your telephone number to Mr. Tanaka.

   Anata no denwa-bangō o Tanaka san ni oshiete moraimashita.
   (The same meaning as 'oshiete itadakimashita but this sentence is politer.)

7. Dare ga anata ni nihongo o oshiete kudasaimashita ka.
   -Yamada sensei ga oshiete kudasaimashita.

Chapter-50

1. Denki o tsukete kudasai.
2. Totsuzen denki ga kiemashita.
3. Hayaku kimete kudasai.
4. Kyōjū ni kono tegami o dashite kudasai.
5. Kowareyasui kara, kore o otosanai yōni ki o tsukete kudasai.
6. Tantō ga kawarimashita.
7. Kono kusuri o nondara, byōki ga naorimasu.

Chapter-51

1. mōshimasu
2. mōshimasu
3. itashimasu
4. Okuni
5. mairimashita
6. irasshaimashita
7. mairimashita
8. Oshigoto
9. shite orimasu
10. meshiagarimasu
11. osuki
12. nasatte irasshaimasu
13. irasshaimasen ka
14. goissho

Chapter-52

1. Nihonjin wa sake o nomuto kao ga akaku narimasu.
   Nihonjin wa sake o nondara kao ga akaku narimasu.
2. Kare ni attara yoroshiku tsutaete kudasai.

3. Tanaka san nara watashi wa yoku shitte imasu.
   Tanaka san dattara watashi wa yoku shitte imasu.

4. Itakereba kono kusuri o nonde kudasai.
   Itakattara kono kusuri o nonde kudasai.
   Itainara kono kusuri o nonde kudasai.
   Itai baai (wa) kono kusuri o nonde kudasai.

5. Yoku kangaeru to kore wa okashii desu.
   Yoku kangaereba kore wa okashii desu.
   Yoku kangaetara kore wa okashii desu.

6. Moshi watashi ga otoko dattara, yakyū no
                               senshu ni natta deshō.
   Moshi watashi ga otoko nara, yakyū no
                               senshu ni natta deshō.

7. Kanojo ga kitara watashi ni shirasete kudasai.
   Kanojo ga kita baai (wa) watashi ni shirasete kudasai.

8. Kaigi ga owattara shokuji ni ikimashō.

Chapter-54

1. Asoko ni tatte iru hito wa dare desu ka.
2. Anata no kaisha ni nihongo ga hanaseru hito ga imasu ka.
3. Ano shiroi uchi ni sunde iru hito o shitte imasu ka.
4. Isu no ue ni oite aru kaban o totte kudasai masen ka.
5. Asoko ni suwatte iru hito wa shachō desu.

INDEX

JAPANESE TO ENGLISH

chōdo ima / just now (doing) -70
chansu / chance - 110
chanto / properly -154
chichi / father -120
chichi / my father -136
chigaimasu / different -101
chikai / near -10
chippu / tip - 110
chotto / little -10

dōshite / why -81
dōzo / please -148
daigaku / university - 51
daigakusei / college student -56
daisuki / like very much -148
daitai / almost -101
dame desu / must -154
dansu / dance -111
dare / who - 5
dashimasu / to post -142
dashimasu / to submit -86
dekireba / if possible -154
dekiru dake / as much as possible -83
demasu / come out -83
demo / demonstration -111
densha / train -70
denwa / telephone - 5
denwabangō / telephone number -27
depāto / department store - 5, 111
dezāto / dessert -111
dezain / design - 101
doa / door -111, 131
doraibā / driver -111
dorobō / thief -120
doru / dollar -111
doyōbi / Saturday -86

eakon / airconditioner -111
eiga / movie -23
eigo / English -10
eki / station - 5,
enerugī / energy -111
enjin / engine -111
enjinia / engineer -148
enpitsu / pencil - 5
ensuto / engine stop, engine failure -111
erīto / elite -111
erebētā / elevator -111, 154
esa / food (for animals) -136

fāsuto-fūdo / fast food -56
fairu / file -17
famikon / video game -111, 116
fasshon / fashion -111
fuben / inconvenient -14
fuku / dress -131
fukuzatsu / complicated -14
furansugo / french-10
furimasu / to rain -47
furonto / front office -111
furui / old -10
furumai masu / to behave -116
fushigi / strange -14
futatsu / two -59
fuyu / winter -49

gakusei / student -51
garēji / garage -111
garasu / sheet glass -111
gasorin / gasoline, petrol -29, -111
gasu / gas -111
genki / cheerful -14
gifuto / gift -131
go-ji / five o'clock -142
go-kiro / 5 kilometers -72
go (suffix) / language - 10
gomi / garbage -95
gomu / rubber -111
gorufu / golf -148
gurūpu / group -154
gurai / about -23
gyūniku / beef -51

hādo / hardware -111
hōmu / platform -111
hōmushikku / homesick -111
hade / flamboyant -14
hai / yes - 5
hairimasu / to enter -81
haiyā / taxi (cab) hired by
    the day -111
haizara / ashtray -139
hajimemasu / to start -64
hakimasu / to wear shoes
    pants etc. -37
hamu / ham -111
han / 30 minutes -23
hana / flower -131
hanashi / talk -39

hanashi / topic -148
hanashimasu / to speak -27
hanbāgu / hamburger -111
handoru / steering wheel -111
hankachi / handkerchief -111
haraimasu / to pay -86
hatarakimasu / to work -23,
hawai / hawaii -136
hayai / fast -10
hayaku / early -59
hebi / snake -116
heddohon / headphone -111
heikin / average -49
heri /helicopter -111
hi / day -136
hikōki / airplane -10
hikimasu / to play (a string
    instrument) -39
hikimasu / to catch (cold) -106
hikkoshi / moving, shifting -124
hikkoshimasu / to move out -59
hima / free -29
hinto / hint -111
Hinzū kyōto / Hindus -95
hiroi / spacious -10
hiru / noon -72
hirugohan / lunch -39
hisho / secretary -120
hito / person -14
hitobito / people -49
hitori / alone -83
hitoride / by oneself -76
hitsuyō / necessary -14
hocchikisu / stapler -111
hoka / other -97
hon / book -5
hondana / book rack -157
hosoi / thin -10
hosutesu / hostess -111

ichi-jikan / for 1 hour -72
ichiban / most -10
ichido / once -77
ichiman-en / ten thousand yen -139
ichimanen satsu / 10,000 yen note -74
ichinichi / for a day -93
ie / house -86
ii (yoi) / good -10
iie / no - 5

iimasu / to say -64
ijō / more than -154
ika / below -95
ikebana / flower arrangement -101
ikimasu / to go -24
ikimasu / to live -154
ikkagetsu / for a month -131
imēji / image -111
imōto / younger sister -67
ima / now -17
indo / India -17
infure / inflation -111
interi / intellectual -111
inu / dog -103
ippai / a glass of -120
Irasuto / illustration -111
iremasu / to install -74
iremasu / to put -81
irimasu / to need -157
iro / colour -61
iroiro / various -17
isogashii / busy -59
isogimasu / to hurry, rush -131
isshūkan / for a week -74
issho / together -120
isu / chair - 5
itai / pain -83
itsumo / always -56
itte kimasu / to go (and come back) -131
iya / unpleasant -14

jōbu / sturdy -14
jōdan / joke -64
jū-ji / 10 o'clock -86
jū-nen / 10 years -59
jūgatsu / October -148
jūhassai / 18 years old -95
jūnigatsu / December -155
jūsu / juice -10, 111
jūyō / important -51
jibun de / by oneself -88
jikan / time -17
jiko / accident -70
jishin / earthquake -17
jisho / dictionary - 5
jugyō / class - 120
jugyōchū / during the class -90
jukkai / 10th floor -93
jumyō / life span -49

229

ki / key -111
kōcha / tea -10
kōen / park -116
kōhi / coffee -10, 111
kōkūken / air ticket -136
kūkō / airport - 5
kūra / cooler, AC -111
kaban / bag - 5
kachō / section chief -52
kaerimasu / to go back -24
kaeshimasu / to return -24
kagi / key -142
kaigi / meeting - 18
kaigishitsu / conference room -90
kaimasu / to keep -103
kaimono / shopping -24
kainushi / keeper, owner (of a pet) -120
kaisha / company - 5
kaji / fire -155
kaji / household work -76
kakemasu / to lock -142
kakemasu / to make (a call) -39
kakimasu / to write -24
kamera / camera - 5, 111
kanai / my wife - 52
kangaemasu / to think -39
kanja / patient -124
kanji / Chinese character -41
kankoku / South Korea -148
kanojo / she -14
kao / face -116
karā / colour -111
kara / from -24
karai / spicy -10
kare / he -14
karendā / calendar -111
karimasu / to borrow -86
karui / light -10
kasa / umbrella - 52
kashimasu / to lend -59
katai / hard -37
katte ikimasu / to buy (and go) -131
katte kimasu / to buy (and
    come back) -131
kawarimasu / to change -142
kaze / cold -106
kazoku / family -148
keibiin / security guard -121
keisatsu / police -121

keitai denwa / cellular phone -74
kekkon / marriage -136
kekkon shimasu / to marry -24
kekkon-shiki / marriage party
    (reception) -101
ken / matter -93
kenkō / health -49
kesa / this morning -18
ki ni irimasu / to like - 61
kiji / article -148
kikai / machine -74
kiken / dangerous -14
kimasu / to come -24
kimemasu / to decide -142
kimochi / feeling -103
kippu / ticket -131
kirai / dislike -14
kirei / beautiful -14
kisetsu / season -67
kitte / stamp -133
kodomo / child -34
koe / voice - 61
koin / coin -111
komarimasu / to be troubled -121
komimasu / to be crowded -101
konban / tonight - 52
konbini / convenience store -111
konde imasu / be crowded - 61
kondo / next time -64
kone / connection, pull -111
kono aida / the other day -116
kono mae / the other day -159
kono mae no / last, previous -79
konogoro / these days -72
konomi / liking, taste -101
konpyūta / computer -37
konsento / power point, socket -111
kopī o shimasu / to copy -131
kopī o torimasu / to take a copy -93
korekara / from now on -24
korobimasu / fall down -70
koroshimasu / to kill -121
kotaemasu / to answer -97
kotoba / word -54
kotoshi / this year -29
kowaremasu / to be broken -142
kowashimasu / to destroy -121
kowashimasu / to upset, ruin -116
kudamono / fruit -72

kuni / country -148
kurīmu / cream -111
kurai / dark -10,
kuruma / car - 5
kusuri / medicine -41
kutsu / shoes -37
kyō / today -18
kyōjū / today itself -142
kyōshitsu / class room - 6
kyū ni / suddenly -121
kyanseru / cancel -112
kyonen / last year - 148

māketto / market - 6
mētoru / metre -112
mō / more -83
mō hitotsu / one more thing -93
mō ichido / once more -84
mō~nai / not anymore -64
mōfu / blanket -59
ma ni aimasu / to be in time -155
machi / city -64
machimasu / to wait -59
made / till -24
mai hōmu / my home -34
maiasa / every morning -24
maiban / every night -24
mainichi / everyday -24,
maitsuki / every month -74
mania / maniac - 112
masukomi / mass communication -112
masuku / mask -112
mawari / surroundings -93
mazui / unpalatable-11
megane / spectacles - 116
meishi / business card -81
mendō / troublesome -56
mendōkusai / troublesome -103
michi / road - 62
mimasu / to check -139
mimasu / to watch -24
minasan / everybody -29
minna / everybody -62
miruku / milk -112
mise / shop -24
misemasu / to show -93
mishin / sewing machine -112
mizu / water -34
mo / also -83

mochimasu / to have -27
mochiron / of course-11
moderu / model -112
modorimasu / to return -88
monitā / monitor -112
mono / thing -18
motte ikimasu / to take
    (something) -131
motte kimasu / to bring
    (something) -131
mudazukai o shimasu / to waste -90
mukaemasu / to receive -88
mukashi / ancient times -81
mukashi / earlier -37
muri shimasu / to force oneself -88
muzukashii / difficult-11

nōto / notebook - 6
nagai / long-11
nakanaka / not easily -37
nakanaka / quite -103
nama / raw -81
nan /~what -6
naorimasu / to get well -107
naraimasu / to learn -27
narimasu / become -29
natsu / summer -41
natsu yasumi / summer vacation -72
nattō / fermented beans (Japanese
    dish) -41
natte kimasu / to become -131
naze / why - 62
nedan / price -101
nega / negative film -112
nekutai / necktie -112, 136
nemasu / to lie down -39
netsu / fever -84
nichiyōbi / Sunday -34
nidoto / never -72
nigai / bitter-11
nigiyaka / noisy, lively -93
nihon / japan-11
nihongo / Japanese language-11
nihonjin / Japanese people-14
nijūgo-sai / 25 years old -56
niku / meat -37
nimotsu / luggage -37
ninzū / number of people -155

niwari / 20% -155
no mae de / in front of -125
noborimasu / to climb -54
noirōze / nervous breakdown -112
nomimasu / to drink -24
nomimono / drinks -131
nyūin shimasu / admit in the hospital -124
nyūsu / news -112
Nyūyōku / New York-11

oboemasu / to remember -88
oboremasu / to drown -70
ochimasu / to fail -133
ochitsukimasu / to relax -155
ōdā / order -112
odorimasu / to dance -37
ofuro / bath -84
ōi / lots of, much -49, 86
oishii / delicious-11
oiwai / gift -136
okane / money -34
okashi / snacks, sweet -54
okashii / strange -155
okayu / porridge -84
okimasu / to get up -24
okimasu / to put -159
okorimasu / to get angry, scold -64,121
okorimasu / to occur -155
okoshimasu / to wake up -142
okuremasu / be delayed -101
okurimasu / to send -131
okusan / (your) wife -131
okyaku san / guest, client -79, 124
omiyage / gift, souvenir -131
omoi / heavy -37
omoshiroi / interesting-11
onaji / same -74
onaka / stomach -84
onaka ga sukimasu / feel hungry - 62
ongaku / music -24
onsen / hot spring -121
oshiemasu / to teach -74
oshimasu / to press -155
osoi / late -52
ōtobai / autobike, motorbike -112, 5
otōsan / father - 29
otōto / younger brother -124
otoko / man, male -155
otoshimasu / to drop -70

owarimasu / to finish -59
oyogimasu / to swim -24
oyu / hot water -131

pāma / perm -112
pātī / party -24
pēji / page -93
pūru / pool -70
pajama / pyjama, night suit -112
pan / bread -112
panikku / panic -112
panku / puncture -112
pantsu / underpants -112
pasokon /personal computer -112
patokā / patrol car -112
patoron / patron -112
pen / pen - 6
penki / paint -112
petto / pet -18
pikunikku / picnic -59, 112
piza / pizza -112
pokeberu /pager -112
poketto / pocket -81
poruno / pornography -112
posuto / mailbox -112
potto / vaccum flask -112
puro / professional -112

rōn / loan -112
raigetsu / next month -29
rainen / next year -64
raishū / next week -101
raito / light -112
rajikase / radio cassette
recorder -34, 112
rajio / radio -112
ranpu / lamp -112
rejā / leisure -112
reji / cash register -112
rekishi / history -139
renshū shimasu / to practice -117
repōto / report -70, 112
resutoran / restaurant - 6
ribingu rūmu / living room -93
rihabiri / rehabilitation -112
rippa / palatial - 62
risaikuru / recycle -112
risuto / list -112
roke / location (for shooting) -112

232

wakarimasu / to understand -59
wakashimasu / to boil -131
wakemasu / to split -155
wanpatān / tereotyped -113
waraimasu / to laugh -124
warui / bad -49
wasuremasu / to forget -84
watashi / I -6

yōbi / the day of the week -101
yōji / work -157
yōkan / Japanese sweet -54
yūbe / last night -97
yūmei / famous -14
yūmoa / humour - 113
yachin / house rent -93
yakusoku / appointment -97
yakyū / baseball -37
yama / mountain -54
yamemasu / to quit, give up -24, 64
yaoya / vegetable store - 6
yarimasu / to do -155
yasai / vegetable -117
yasashii / gentle -14

yasui / cheap-11
yasumi / holiday -47
yasumimasu / to have a break -24
yatoimasu / to employ -155
yatto / finally -37
yobidashimasu / to call, summon -121
yobimasu / to call -27
yoku / often -76
yoku / well -47
yoroshiku onegai shimasu / Nice
    to meet you -149
yoru / night -27
yotto / yacht -113
yukai / jolly -14
yuki / snow -67
yukkuri / slowly -27

zannen / unfortunate -14
zasshi / magazine - 6
zehi / by all means - 52
zenbu / all, everything -88
zenzen nai / not at all -11
zubon / trousers -113
zutto / throughout -24

ENGLISH TO JAPANESE

5 kilometers / go-kiro -72
7 o'clock / shichi-ji -56
10 o'clock / jū-ji -86, 148
10th floor / jukkai -93
10 years / jū-nen -59
18 years old / jūhassai -95
25 years old / nijūgo-sai -56
30 minutes / han -23
30 years old / sanjussai -29
10,000 yen note / ichimanen satsu -74
20% / niwari -155

a glass of / ippai -120
a little, bit / sukoshi -29
a little while ago / sakki -18
a lot of / takusan -72
about / gurai -23
about / tsuite -49
accelerator / akuseru -110
accident / jiko -70
admit in the hospital / nyūin
    shimasu -124
age / toshi -149
air ticket / kōkūken -136
airconditioner / eakon -111
airplane / hikōki -10
airport / kūkō -5
alcohol / arukōru -110
all, everything / zenbu -88
almost / daitai -10
alone / hitori -83
also / mo -83
always / itsumo -56
America / Amerika -98
ancient times / mukashi -81
animation / anime -110
another / ato -131
apartment / apāto - 67, 110
appointment / apointo -110
appointment / yakusoku -97
April / shigatsu -131
around there / sono hen -98
article / kiji -148
as many (much) as possible
    dekirudake -83
as usual / aikawarazu -148
ashtray / haizara -139
autobike, motorbike / ōtobai -112

average / heikin -49
bad / warui -49
bag / kaban -5
ball / bōru -110
ball point pen / bōrupen - 5
barber / tokoya -6
baseball / yakyū -37
bath / ofuro -84
bazaar / bazā -110
be crowded / konde imasu -61
be delayed / okuremasu -101
beautiful / kirei -14
become / narimasu -29
bed / beddo -110
beef / gyūniku -51
beer / bīru -93, 110
below / ika -95
bike / baiku -110
birthday / tanjōbi -59
biscuit / bisuketto -110
bitter / nigai -11
blanket / mōfu -59
bonus / bōnasu -110
book / hon -5
book rack / hondana -157
bread / pan -112
break / burēki -110
breakfast / asagohan -27
bright / akarui -10
bucket / baketsu -110
building / biru -110
bullet train / shinkansen -131
bus / basu -59, 110
bus stop / basutei -5
business card / meishi -81
business hotel / bijinesu hoteru -110
business trip / shucchō -86
business,work / shigoto -39
businessman / bijinesu man -110
busy / isogashii -59
butter / batā -110
button / botan -110, 154
by all means / zehi -52
by chance / battari -154
by oneself / hitoride -76
by oneself / jibun de -88
bye bye / bai bai -110

Japanese public bath / sentō -77
Japanese rice wine / sake -24
Japanese sweet / yōkan -54
Japanese tea ceremony / sadō -101
joke / jōdan -64
jolly / yukai -14
juice / jūsu -10, 111
June / rokugatsu -49
just now (doing) / chōdo ima -70
just now (finished) / tatta ima -70, 133
just now / tadaima -149

keeper, owner (of a pet) / kainushi -120
key / kī -111
key / kagi -142
kind / shinsetsu -14

lamp / ranpu -112
language / go (suffix) -10
last night / sakuya -117
last night / yūbe -97
last year / kyonen -148
last, previous / kono mae no -79
late / osoi -52
later / ato de -59
leisure / rejā -112
letter / tegami -24
library / toshokan -107
life span / jumyō -49
light / karui -10
light / raito -112
like / suki -14
like very much / daisuki -148
liking, taste / konomi -101
list / risuto -112
little / chotto -10
living room / ribingu rūmu -93
lots of / ōi -49
loan / rōn -112
location (for shooting) / roke -112
lock / rokku -112
London / Rondon -47
long / nagai -11
luggage / nimotsu -37
lunch / hirugohan -39

machine / kikai -74
magazine / zasshi -6, 93
mailbox / posuto -112

man, male / otoko -155
maniac / mania -112
manual / setsumeisho -97
market / māketto -6
marriage / kekkon -136
marriage party (reception) /
  kekkon-shiki -101
mask / masuku -112
mass communication / masukomi -112
matter / ken -93
meal / shokuji -39
meat / niku -37
medicine / kusuri -41
meeting / kaigi -18
mercedes / bentsu -155
metre / mētoru -112
milk / miruku -112
model / model -112
money / okane -34
monitor / monitā -112
more / mō -83
more than / ijō -154
most / ichiban -10
most of time, usually / taitei -149
mountain / yama -54
movie / eiga -23
moving, shifting / hikkoshi -124
Mr, Ms. / san -6
much /ōi -86
music / ongaku -24
must / dame desu -154
my father / chichi -136
my home / mai hōmu -34
my husband / shujin -52
my wife / kanai -52

near / chikai -10
necessary / hitsuyō -14
necktie / nekutai -112, 136
negative film / nega -112
neighbour / tonari -142
nervous breakdown / noirōze -112
never / nidoto -72
new / atarashii -10
New York / Nyūyōku -11
news / nyūsu -112
newspaper / shinbun -6
next month / raigetsu -29

salaried worker / sarariman -112
same / onaji -74
Saturday / doyōbi -86
sauce / sōsu -113
school bus / sukūru basu -113
season / kisetsu -67
seat belt / shīto beruto -86
secretary / hisho -120
section chief / kachō -52
securityguard / keibiin -121
service / sābisu -112
sewing machine / mishin -112
sex / sekkusu -112
she / kanojo -14
sheet glass / garasu -111
shirt / shatsu -81
shoes / kutsu -37
shop / mise -24
shopping / kaimono -24
shower / shawā -27
sick / byōki -47
silk / shiruku -136
slightly / sukoshi -11
slipper / surippa -113
slowly / yukkuri -27
small, cramped / semai -11
smart / sumāto -14, 113
snacks, sweet / okashi -54
snake / hebi -116
snow / yuki -67
so / sō -6
soccer / sakkā -112
society / shakai -101
software / sofuto -113
song / uta -39
soon / sorosoro -86
soon / sugu -59
South Korea / kankoku -148
soya beans cake / tōfu -149
spacious / hiroi -10
spectacles / megane -116
speed / supīdo -113
spicy / karai -10
sports / supōtsu -113
staff / sutaffu -113
staff, employee / shain -124
stamina / sutamina -113
stamp / kitte -133
stapler / hocchikisu -111
station / eki - 5

steak / sutēki -41, 113
steam / suchīmu -113
steering wheel / handoru -111
stereotyped / wanpatān -113
stomach / onaka -84
strange / fushigi -14
strange / okashii -155
strike (work) / sutoraiki (suto) -113
student / gakusei -51
sturdy / jōbu -14
style / sutairu -113
suddenly / kyū ni -121
sugar / satō -142
suit / sūtsu -113
summer / natsu -41
summer vacation / natsu yasumi -72
sunday / nichiyōbi -34
supermarket, superimpose, subtitles /
    sūpā -6, 113
surroundings / mawari -93
sweater / sētā -113
sweet / amai -10

T.V / terebi -6, 113
table, desk / tsukue -6, 113
take (a shower) / abimasu -27
take (photoes) / torimasu -124
talk / hanashi -39
tape recorder / tēpu rekōdā -34
taxi (cab) hired by the day / haiyā -111
tea / kōcha -10
teacher / sensei -27
telephone / denwa - 5
telephone number / denwabangō -27
ten thousand yen / ichiman-en -139
terminal / tāminaru -113
terrorism / tero -113
text / tekisuto -113
thank you / arigtō -54
the day of the week / yōbi -101
the other day / kono aida -116
the other day / kono mae -159
theme / tēma -113
then / sorekara -84
these days / konogoro -72
thesis / ronbun -133
thief / dorobō -120
thin / hosoi -10
thing / mono -18
this morning / kesa -18

241

this year / kotoshi -29
throughout / zutto -24
ticket / kippu -131
till / made -24
time / jikan -17
time card / taimu kādo -74
tip / chippu - 110
to abandon, throw away / sutemasu -121
to answer / kotaemasu -97
to appear (an exam) / ukemasu -124
to arrest / taiho shimasu -121
to ask a question / shitsumon shimasu -93
to avoid / sakemasu -117
to be broken / kowaremasu -142
to be crowded / komimasu -101
to be in time / ma ni aimasu -155
to behave / furumai masu-116
to be tired / tsukaremasu -131
to be transferred / tenkin shimasu -74
to be troubled / komarimasu -121
to become / natte kimasu -131
to boil / wakashimasu -131
to borrow / karimasu -86
to bring (something) / motte kimasu -131
to bring (a person along) / tsurete kimasu -131
to buy (and come back) / katte kimasu -131
to buy (and go) / katte ikimasu -131
to call / yobimasu -27
to call, summon / yobidashimasu -121
to change / kawarimasu -142
to check / mimasu -139
to clean a place / sōji shimasu -79
to climb / noborimasu -54
to close / shimemasu -131
to collect / atsumemasu -133
to come / kimasu -24
to come out / demasu -83
to convey / tsutaemasu -155
to copy / kopī o shimasu -131
to dance / odorimasu -37
to decide / kimemasu -142
to destroy / kowashimasu -121
to die / shinimasu -70
to do / shimasu -24
to do / yarimasu -155

to drink / nomimasu -24
to drop / otoshimasu -70
to drown / oboremasu -70
to eat (and go) / tabete ikimasu -131
to employ / yatoimasu -155
to enter / hairimasu -81
to exercise / undō shimasu -56
to explain / setsumei shimasu -64
to fail / ochimasu -133
to fasten / shimemasu -86
to finish / owarimasu -59
to force oneself / muri shimasu -88
to forget / wasuremasu -84
to get angry, scold / okorimasu -64,121
to get up / okimasu -24
to get well / naorimasu -107
to give / agemasu -81
to give up / yamemasu -64
to go (and come back) / itte kimasu -131
to go / ikimasu -24
to go back / kaerimasu -24
to guide / annai shimasu -148
to have / mochimasu -27
to have a break / yasumimasu -24
to help / tetsudaimasu -76
to hurry, rush / isogimasu -131
to install / iremasu -74
to introduce / shōkai shimasu -139
to keep / kaimasu -103
to kill / koroshimasu -121
to know / shirimasu -27
to know / shitte imasu -117
to laugh / waraimasu -124
to learn / naraimasu -27
to lend / kashimasu -59
to lie down / nemasu -39
to like / ki ni irimasu -61
to live / ikimasu -154
to live / sumimasu -131
to lock / kakemasu -142
to make / tsukurimasu -117
to make (a call) / kakemasu -39
to marry / kekkon shimasu -24
to move out / hikkoshimasu -59
to need / irimasu -157
to occur / okorimasu -155
to open / akemasu -131
to pass, to get / torimasu -139
to pay / haraimasu -86